Kingdom of

Fife

40 Coast and Country Walks

The author and publisher have made every effort to ensure that the information in this publication is accurate, and accept no responsibility whatsoever for any loss, injury or inconvenience experienced by any person or persons whilst using this book.

published by
pocket mountains ltd
The Old Church, Annanside, Moffat
Dumfries & Galloway DG10 9HB
www.pocketmountains.com

ISBN: 978-0-9554548-3-7

Text copyright © Dan Bailey

Photography copyright © Dan Bailey

Printed in Poland (REP2016)

Introduction

The Kingdom may be small, but it is perfectly formed. This is a county of contrasts, its personality split between the bustling industrial south and the rural north and east. Full of interesting nooks and unexpected beauty, this varied corner of Scotland manages to pack in a little of everything. Urban attractions include St Andrews, centre of medieval church power and ancient seat of learning, and Dunfermline, erstwhile Scottish capital. Within a stone's throw of the towns are long stretches of unspoilt coastline, woodland walks, characterful hills, grand country estates and friendly old villages. Fife boasts some of the most notable historic buildings in Scotland, including the palaces of Culross and Falkland, and the abbeys at Dunfermline and Inchcolm. Centuries of industry have left a fascinating heritage of their own – quarry pits, viaducts, limekilns and crumbling chimney stacks.

Inland Fife holds many places of interest. Highlights include the Lomond Hills, an island-like massif of dramatic steep escarpments and wide open spaces; bird-rich Loch Leven (strictly speaking in a different county, but it's right on our doorstep); and the far-eastern Ochils overlooking the Firth of Tay – little known hills, yet beautiful. But perhaps Fife's real trump card is its coastline. From the rocky inlets and islets of the Forth to the peaceful East Neuk and the wide sands of Tentsmuir, the smell of the sea is never far

away. With hills at its back and three sides lapped by water, the Kingdom does have a distinct, almost island-like character – as reflected in its maritime history. The ideal way to explore it all is on foot.

Fife is renowned for its pristine, sandy and, at many times of year, near-empty beaches. Add historic fishing villages and castles, lush farmland and sweeping sea views and you've got the makings of a pretty special walk. Linking the iconic Forth and Tay bridges via every seaside settlement from Culross to Newport-on-Tay, the Fife Coastal Path showcases the county at its best. Yet this superb route is a relatively unsung star in Scotland's long-distance footpath firmament, deserving greater recognition. It would take about a week to walk the entire route, but in this volume it is broken down into seven single-day edited highlights.

A brief history of Fife

You don't have to walk far to see signs of Fife's long history. The landscape has been shaped by millennia of human activity from Stone Age hunter gatherers of 8000 years ago to the present; evidence is everywhere. Picts, Romans, Norse, Scots, Northumbrians and Normans all passed this way over the years – not always peacefully. Prehistoric hillforts, medieval castles and World War relics bear testament to bygone struggles.

Successive settlers brought their own ways of speaking to Fife, and today's place names echo languages long since vanished. Pitmedden and Aberdour are Pictish in origin; Dunfermline stems from Gaelic. By the early Middle Ages the dominant tongue here was Scots, a relation of Old English that evolved into something quite distinct from the sort of English spoken down south. This rich dialect (or more correctly a set of related regional dialects) thrives to this day in Lowland Scotland, and is strongly reflected in the street names, literature and everyday speech of Fife.

The Kingdom has a long association with Scottish royalty (hence Fife's nickname). Dunfermline served for a spell as the capital of Scotland, while the nearby Falkland Palace was a favourite holiday home for generations of royals. Fife nobility had enviable influence and status in medieval Scotland, and the Kingdom enjoyed a similar position in the ecclesiastical realm too. The archbishopric of St Andrews was for centuries the most important seat of church power in the country. The shrine to St Andrew, from which the town got its name, was said to contain genuine relics of this celebrated apostle of Christ, becoming a prime destination for religious pilgrims from as early as the 10th century. St Andrew was later rebranded as the patron saint of Scotland, a powerful symbol of the independence of Scottish church and crown from their English rivals. Pilgrimage routes homed in on St Andrews from all corners of the country, a religiously-motivated transport infrastructure funded by pious royalty and nobility. Place names such as Queensferry and Earlsferry reflect this history.

St Andrews can also boast Scotland's first university, and the third oldest in the English-speaking world, founded as early as 1413. The beautiful quads of St Salvator's College and St Mary's College attest to the ancient heritage of this venerable institution, the alma mater of centuries' worth of illustrious scientists, churchmen, politicians and writers.

A political, religious and intellectual powerhouse, Fife has been no slouch in economic terms either. Thriving on sea trade and fishing, prosperous villages grew up along Fife's coast, the most important of which were established as royal burghs – communities enjoying a degree of autonomy and parliamentary representation, and even special rights on foreign trade. Kinghorn and Crail were granted such status as early as the 12th century. These ports had strong links with continental Europe, as evidenced today in their distinctive Flemish-influenced architecture. In a sense Fife was more outward-looking in this period than much of Scotland, perhaps thanks to its eastward cultural orientation and its physical geography as a maritime peninsula relatively isolated from the rest of the country. This is reflected in the old saying 'Bid farewell to Scotland, and cross to Fife'.

Motorways, railways and bridges have since made the crossing rather easier, though the isolated East Neuk still retains a subtle sense of separation.

The Industrial Revolution of the 18th and 19th centuries brought new waves of development to Fife as the urban population exploded in tandem with a boom in coal mining, textiles, papermaking and boatbuilding. A huge dislocation occurred as the centre of demographic and economic gravity shifted from the agricultural north and east of Fife to the expanding towns of the south and west – laying down a pattern of settlement that has persisted into the 21st century.

Once resource-rich, the area has faced challenges in recent decades. Fishing and the sea trade are no more, coal mining has collapsed, and traditional heavy industry is experiencing ongoing problems. Despite these changes, manufacturing still accounts for a greater share of the Fife economy than the Scottish average. The future is uncertain, but one thing is for sure – Fife is rich in human resources, and we will always need unspoilt places to walk and unwind. Fife's coastline and countryside are beautiful and varied – get out there and enjoy them.

About this guide

There is something for everyone in Fife. The selected walks span a range of difficulty from 1km strolls on level paths to 28km day-long hikes over rough hilly ground. As well as a breakdown of distance and ascent for each route, notes are included about the terrain the walk covers; this should help people of all abilities find something suitable. Less ambitious walkers and parents with buggies or young children should pay particular attention to the terrain information provided here. Since everyone has their own level of fitness and agility, it's difficult to give accurate time estimates for any route. Walk times in this book err on the generous side, but they should only be taken as a rough guide. Compass directions are approximate; left and right are relative to the direction of travel. A track is something one might be able to drive a Landrover down (not that you should); a path isn't.

Access

Scotland enjoys some of the most liberal access legislation in the world. The public right to use open hill country, privately owned or not, is enshrined in law under the Land Reform (Scotland) Act of 2003. It's worth noting, however, that legal access still comes with strings attached. The Scottish Outdoor Access Code refers pointedly to 'responsible access', which is fundamentally just a formal term for common sense and consideration. To abide by the spirit of the legislation do not enter private gardens, don't walk on arable fields (use the unplanted margins if you must), don't camp within sight of houses, try to pick a route that climbs a minimum of fences and walls (where this is unavoidable be extremely careful not to cause any damage), keep dogs under close control (on a lead if sheep or cows are around), don't persecute livestock and steer clear of any forestry, shooting or farming activities. In contrast to the wide, wild expanses of the Highlands, the Kingdom is populous and intensively farmed, so walkers should make every effort to play by these simple rules.

What to take

The few genuine hillwalking routes described in this book cover some rough ground, and can leave walkers exposed to the elements for several hours. These are best treated as you would a mountain day in the Highlands; wear walking boots, and carry a rucksack with spare warm and waterproof layers and plenty of food and drink. Even in sunny Fife poor weather can suddenly close in, restricting hilltop visibility to as little as a few metres. In these sticky situations a map, a compass and the ability to use them all rapidly take on the status of utter essentials. On a similar note, in the short days of winter it may pay to carry a torch in case your trip takes longer than expected. Finishing a route in pitch darkness using just the senses of smell and touch isn't as fun as it sounds.

The maps in this book are a guide only, and on longer rural walks something more detailed is usually welcome. 1:25,000 scale maps are generally best at showing the intricate wiggles of footpaths through farmland, the presence of fences and so forth, so the information box for each route details the appropriate Ordnance Survey sheet at that scale.

Walking with children

While pavements and well-made paths are easily negotiated with an all-terrain buggy, steep hills, deep mud and stiles tend to hamper wheeled progress. If you're thinking of doing any but the gentlest of these walks with a baby or smaller toddler then a backpack is probably a better option. Make sure the wee ones have adequate sun protection in summer and plenty of warm stuff in winter (or this being Scotland, both in either season) – if they're being carried they're effectively immobile, and more vulnerable to the cold. At that awkward stage when they're too heavy to lug about but too small to walk in any meaningful adult sense then you may have to settle for a snail's pace with endless distractions and diversions. It may be hard to coax older children away from their games consoles, but if they can be prised out of their troglodytic obesity-inducing torpor they'll be all the better for the fresh air and exercise. Perhaps try engaging their imagination by making an adventure out of the day's walk, clambering on rocks, playing pooh sticks or building a den in the woods. Why not take them wild camping on the hills or seal spotting at Tentsmuir? Walking isn't something to take too seriously; we're all doing it for fun after all. Hands-on learning about the natural world should be a big part of every child's upbringing; the wetter and muddier, the better.

Walking with dogs

Unlike kids, mutts need to be kept under strict control in the countryside. If there is any chance they'll disturb livestock or wildlife then put them on a tight lead. It ought to go without saying that in parks and along popular trails dog owners should scrupulously clean up after their pets, bagging and binning the offending substances; sadly there always seems to be someone willing to leave a bag of poo hanging from the nearest branch.

Transport

It's probably fair to assume that people who like walking also have an affection for the countryside, and might prefer to minimise the environmental footprint of their weekend trips. So how are you getting to and from your walk? Cars are convenient of course, and it'd be a hypocritical guidebook writer that condemned their use; but if you are driving then it's at least worth buying into the current vogue for lift sharing if possible, with the knock-on benefit that you'll share fuel costs. This being densely populated Fife, however, rather than the outer reaches of Sutherland, you're rarely that far from a train station or bus stop. Where a practical choice exists, each route chapter highlights public transport availability; indeed, some routes have been planned on the premise that walkers will be coming on the bus or train. Public transport information is available at www.travelinescotland.com

Wildlife

There are several nature reserves and Sites of Special Scientific Interest (SSSI) in Fife and the surrounding area; the most notable include the teeming bird havens of Loch Leven and the Eden Estuary, and the seal-spotters' paradise of Tentsmuir. But besides the obvious hotspots wildlife thrives in all corners, from foxes in a suburban garden to the occasional spectacular whale or dolphin sighting in the Forth. Species to look out for on the coast include common and grey seals, porpoises, fulmars, shags, puffins, eider ducks, herons and guillemots. Inland, walkers might spot pink-footed and greylag geese, several varieties of duck, roe deer, red squirrels and even otters. Buzzards are often seen sitting on fenceposts – but if it's really impressive raptors you're after then they don't come much bigger than the white-tailed sea eagle; since the RSPB began an East Coast reintroduction programme, sightings of this majestic bird have become fairly regular in Fife. Watch the skies.

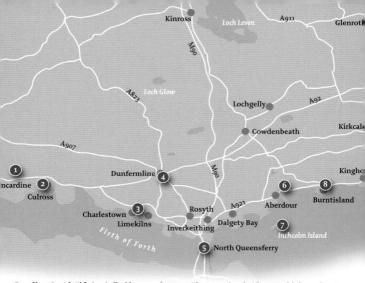

Kinross · Loch Leven · A911 · Glenrot

M90

A823 · Loch Glow

Lochgelly · A92

Cowdenbeath · Kirkcal

A907

(1)

(2) ncardine · Culross

Dunfermline · **(4)** · M90

(3) Charlestown · Limekilns · Rosyth · A921 · Aberdour · **(6)** · **(8)** · Burntisland · Kingho

Inverkeithing · Dalgety Bay

Firth of Forth · **(7)** · Inchcolm Island

(5) North Queensferry

Bustling South Fife is girdled by an urban belt stretching from Inverkeithing and Rosyth through Dunfermline, erstwhile capital of Scotland, and industrial Cowdenbeath to Kirkcaldy, the Kingdom's most populous town.

This has for centuries been a region of hard toil – coal mines, factories, shipyards and docks. The iconic Forth Bridges are symbolic of this engineering excellence and provide one of the great walks of the region. While there's an impressive scale to contemporary plant too, the utilitarian modern aesthetic of petrochemical works and power stations isn't to everyone's taste, and the selected walks in this area tend to steer away from them. But it would be hard to walk anywhere in this part of Fife without getting an insight into its fascinating industrial heritage.

The quarries, bridges and kilns of past ages have their own sort of beauty to them, the chimneys belching black smoke no longer as nature reclaims the crumbling relics.

Other walks here take in the best of the town centres and urban parks – Dunfermline's ancient heart, historic Inverkeithing and North Queensferry, and Kirkcaldy's superb Beveridge Park. But, as ever, there's much more to this diverse area than towns and industry. Surprisingly unspoilt pockets of countryside are everywhere, offering walks in rolling fields, hills and woods, along stretches of scenic Forth coastline and through quaint old villages. South Fife is full of striking contrasts – urban and rural, industrial and agricultural, ancient and contemporary.

Dunfermline Abbey ▸

The South of the Kingdom

Secrets of Devilla Forest

**Distance 6km Time 3 hours
Terrain maintained trails and forest
tracks, with short rougher sections
Map OS Explorer 367 Access regular bus
to Culross or Kincardine from
Dunfermline**

**Deep among the attractive Scots pines of
Devilla Forest you'll find hidden lochs,
fascinating archaeology and elusive
wildlife from red squirrels to otters.**

From the main Devilla Forest car park by
the A985 pass an information sign to head
west on the Red Squirrel Trail, a purpose-
made footpath winding through open
pinewoods more reminiscent of the
Highlands than Fife. After nearly 1km reach
the little woodland pool of Bordie Loch,
where the path splits. Loop up and left
away from the loch onto an open area with
views to the Forth and Longannet Power
Station. Here look left for the Standard
Stone, a plinth of sandstone thought to
have been the base for a wooden cross
or gallows.

Continue along the trail until it begins to
curve back on itself (to make a loop of
Bordie Loch). Here leave the made path for
a hard-to-follow unofficial route heading
west for several hundred rough metres to
join a forestry track. If you need something
to aim for, a row of telegraph poles show
the line of the track. Turn right on the track
to reach a crossroads, marked by a
fingerpost. Here go left, roughly west, to
meet a double row of huge powerlines that
run in a swathe of open ground cutting
through the heart of the forest. The track
bends right, following the powerlines to
reach a T-junction.

Turn left here to re-enter the pines. After
a few hundred metres look out on the right

◄ In Devilla Forest

for a turn-off signed Curling Pond, Moor Loch and Danish Camp. Muddy in places, this unofficial trail weaves through the woods to reach the shore of Moor Loch, a wildlife haven fringed with dense thickets. Following the shoreline rightwards the path soon becomes a tunnel through rhododendrons, with water on either side – the course of an old dam. At its far end is the Danish Camp. Earthworks marked on the map, and clearly visible on the ground, these banks and ditches were a fort reputedly used by Vikings, but probably Roman or Pictish in origin.

The path goes left around the perimeter of the fort, then crosses a footbridge over a little burn. Now head roughly north through the woods between Moor Loch and the powerline – a short section where the trail is easily lost – to reach a forestry track near two of the pylons. Turn right onto this (roughly east) to re-enter the woods. Go straight ahead at the first split and then straight on again at a crossroads, following a sign for Cycleway Coastal rather than Car Park. At the next junction go right, where the trail winds uphill to reach a long straight section. This leads in about 1km to another crossroads, where the car park is signed on the right. Ignoring a couple of turn-offs, follow this track back to the start.

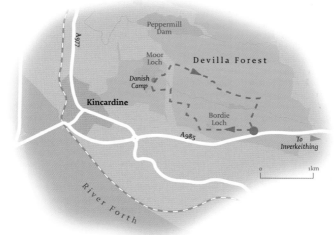

Culross Palace in wonderland

Distance 3km **Time** allow at least 3 hours to do justice to the historic buildings **Terrain** pavements and field tracks, occasionally muddy **Map** OS Explorer 367 **Access** regular buses to Culross from Dunfermline, via High Valleyfield

Town-and-country sightseeing around Scotland's most intact 16th- to 18th-century settlement, including the unique palace and its period terraced garden.

Despite a view over the water to the smoking Grangemouth oil refinery, tranquil Culross seems almost untouched by the modern world. In earlier times, however, this was the centre of Scotland's coal mining industry. The first mine was dug here in 1575 and in 1595 the 'Moat Pit', the first undersea mine in the world, was constructed, running from Culross out under the Firth of Forth.

There were also thriving coal tar and

salt panning industries, and for a time Culross became a busy exporting port. The prevalence of red roof tiles in Fife is thought to be a result of Dutch collier ships returning to Culross with them as ballast. The ancient royal burgh fell into decline in the 18th century, however, and today its fine buildings and narrow cobbled wynds are preserved in a sort of time capsule, thanks to the work of the National Trust for Scotland.

From the coastal car park just west of the village centre follow your nose to the distinctive mustard-coloured Culross Palace, a grand 16th-century merchant's house. The palace is open from March to October, while its lovingly restored terraced garden is open year round. Guided tours run hourly from the palace to the Town House and The Study, two other superb landmarks.

Leaving the palace, pass the Town

◀ Colourful Culross

House with its unusual tower, then turn left up the cobbled Back Causeway to the Mercat Cross, standing in a little square outside The Study. Walk steeply up Tanhouse Brae and Kirk Street to reach Culross Abbey, founded by the Cistercians in 1217. The extensive ruins are on several levels, from the vaulted basement to the more recent parish church with its huge tower.

Once you've 'done' the abbey continue north along the road, soon turning left at a speed limit sign to pick up a footpath along a field edge. Cross another road and go straight on along a field track to reach a track junction. Turn right (signposted for West Kirk) to follow a narrow path between hedges, then turn left onto a wider track leading to West Kirk, a spooky isolated ruined church and graveyard with many faded carvings.

From the kirk continue west on a muddy track, cross the old tree-lined drive to the privately-owned Dunimarle Castle, going straight on as indicated by a sign. From here a longer walk could be made through nearby Devilla Forest, but the quickest way back is to turn left at the next signpost (marked Culross via Dunimarle). A path now leads south through woods, heading towards the Forth. Skirting right of the castle, descend to the coast road just west of Culross. Cross over onto a tarmac path that runs parallel to the shore and the railway; Culross is five minutes away.

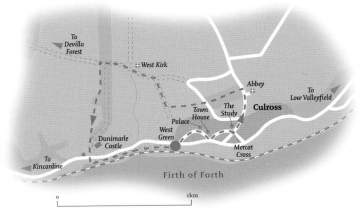

Charlestown and Limekilns

Distance 7km **Time 2 hours** **Terrain level
pavements and paths with a short stretch
of uneven ground along the disused
railway west of Charlestown (this section
of the walk could be avoided)
Map OS Explorer 367 Access regular buses
from Dunfermline**

**Two conservation villages, fascinating
industrial heritage, a grand country
estate and an attractive stroll along a
short stretch of the newly extended Fife
Coastal Path.**

From the seafront car park just west of
Limekilns village centre, walk west on the
Promenade, a row of old houses backed by
wooded sandstone crags. Just beyond the
welcoming Ship Inn and the war
memorial, the road forks. Stay left on Salt
Pans, regaining the shore at the old
harbour. Turn left onto a grassy path,

following the man-made shoreline around
to Charlestown's once bustling main
harbour. The road continues west past a
row of old limekilns, archways in a massive
stone façade. Back in the 1750s this was
cutting edge industrial plant, producing up
to a third of all Scotland's quicklime (used
in farming and building), which was
shipped out from the adjacent wharves.

Go straight on through modern housing
to pick up a wooded footpath along the
course of a disused railway above the stone
sea wall. Where the rusting tracks split,
keep left. Just before reaching naval
buildings at DM Crombie, turn right to
ascend a concrete stairway, crossing a
bridge over the railway and continuing
uphill on a woodland path. Heading back
east, the path soon meets a surfaced track.
Go left to reach a public road and turn
right back into Charlestown. At the post

◀ High and dry in Limekilns harbour

office bear right to reach the village green, ringed by distinctive terraces of single-storey cottages. Founded in the 18th century by local grandee Charles, 5th Earl of Moray, Charlestown was a model village built to house miners, quarrymen and kiln workers.

Beyond the far end of the village green is a gated entrance to the beautiful woods of Broomhall Estate. Access is restricted during pheasant shoots, so call the estate office for current information. A track leads into the woods, soon curving inland through the mounds of a disused quarry. Follow an arrowed route skirting left of the fenced grounds of the grand Broomhall House; cross a field in front of the house, passing through a gate onto a drive.

Turning left, follow the drive through the estate grounds, staying right to pass a cottage and soon reaching the A985. Follow the pavement right, ignoring the turn-off for Dunfermline Road (an optional shortcut back into Limekilns), and continue along the A985 to reach a paved cycle track on the right, also signed for Limekilns. This dog-legs through fields close to Rosyth naval base to reach the sea. Follow the shore west around shallow sandy bays, passing the ancient ruin of Rosyth Church to reach Limekilns again. The sea port for medieval Dunfermline, this pretty little village has a long maritime heritage; it's worth wandering down Main Street to have a look at the historic houses of Academy Square.

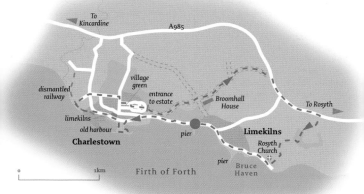

15

Historic Dunfermline

Distance 3km **Time** the sights deserve at least 2 hours **Terrain** pavements and tarmac, with one short, steep flight of stone steps (optional) **Map** OS Explorer 367; but more useful is a free map from the tourist information centre **Access** the train station is several blocks away, but the new bus station is very close to the High Street

Short on distance but not in interest, this walk offers superb historical sightseeing in Scotland's ancient capital, plus one of the best town centre parks in Scotland.

Start at Dunfermline bus station or the nearby car park off Chalmers Street. First make for the tourist information centre on the corner of the High Street and Kirkgate, just opposite the grand turreted City Chambers; pick up your free city plan here. Head down Kirkgate, turning left onto

Maygate to reach the pink stone Abbot House, built in the 15th century and now an excellent visitor centre. It is well worth the modest entry charge. Now pass through the ornamental garden behind the house to enter the grounds of Dunfermline Abbey, founded in 1128 and the resting place of several medieval kings.

The 19th-century square tower of the Abbey Church brashly proclaims 'King Robert the Bruce' in carved stone to celebrate his final resting place under a magnificent brass grave marker inside; the simple pillared Norman interior of the Old Church is much more subtle and interesting. Across the graveyard the massive ruined facades of the Refectory and adjacent Palace are also worth a close look.

From the arched west door of the Abbey Church, walk left down cobbled Monastery

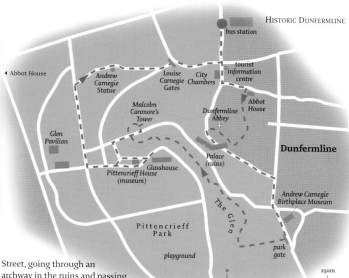

Street, going through an archway in the ruins and passing a war memorial to leave the pedestrianised area. Turn right, heading downhill to the Andrew Carnegie Birthplace Museum on Moodie Street (free admission), a humble cottage where the famous 19th-century millionaire industrialist and philanthropist came into the world. Just downhill through a car park is an entrance to Pittencrieff Park, gifted to the city by Carnegie in 1903.

A path winds downhill to a children's playground. Turn right to follow The Glen with its little burn snaking between steep wooded banks. The path crosses a bridge over the burn by a weir, continuing along the far bank past a sign marking Wallace's Well. Recrossing the burn, carry on along a concrete walkway under a double-tiered bridge to reach a T-junction by a waterfall.

Ascend right to a broad avenue, then kink hard left, climbing smooth stone steps onto a knoll topped with the ruined stump of Malcolm Canmore's Tower. Back at the broad avenue, turn right to cross the double-tiered bridge, then left to reach Pittencrieff House, a historic stone mansion now housing a free museum. Next door are some interesting old glasshouses.

Continue west to a fountain, then turn right past the art deco Glen Pavilion. If you've got kids in tow, look out for an old steam train here. Follow a tree-lined walk, then branch right past a statue of Andrew Carnegie on a grassy rise. Leave the park through the imposing iron gates at the foot of the High Street.

Bridging the Forth

Distance 8km **Time** 3 hours **Terrain** level
pavements and a leg on a clear well-signed
shoreline footpath; crossing the Forth
Road Bridge feels very exposed in wet and
windy weather **Map** OS Explorer 367
Access starting and finishing at train
stations on the busy Fife Circle and
Edinburgh to Dundee line; it is possible
to cut the walk short at North
Queensferry station

**This walk visits two old ports linked
by engineering icons from three
centuries – the Victorian Forth Bridge,
the 20th-century Forth Road Bridge
and the more recently completed
Queensferry Crossing.**

Inverkeithing was granted royal burgh
status as early as the 12th century, and
several historic buildings can still be seen.
From the train station head onto Church
Street and go left to pass the parish church,
parts of which date from the 15th century.

Opposite is 17th-century Fordell's Lodging,
turreted in classic Scottish baronial style.
At the north end of the wide High Street is
the Mercat Cross, thought to date to
around 1400, and at the south end is the
chunky stone 14th-century Friary. The High
Street soon becomes Hope Street; stay on
this to go past allotments and under a
railway bridge. Just before a much bigger
rail bridge go left down Ferryhills Road
(signed for the Fife Coastal Path), then left
again onto Cruickness Road, passing the
harbourside scrapyard. Follow marker
signs for the Coastal Path, which leads
around a quarry to reach the mouth of the
harbour, where the path swings abruptly
right. Scenes of gritty industry are left
behind, and the route now follows the
bouldery shore through coastal woodland.

Beyond two secluded houses the track
becomes a narrower path, which soon
reaches the dark sand bay of Port Laing.
Passing more large houses continue along

◀ The Forth Bridge

the wooded coast, the path now climbing steadily to enter Carlingnose Point Wildlife Reserve, notable for its lime-rich grassland. Beside the old quarry workings the route kinks right onto the gorse-covered headland above North Queensferry, with a close-up view of the awesome Forth Rail Bridge, a marvel of Victorian engineering for which at least 73 workers paid with their lives. Go under the massive stone bridge piers to enter North Queensferry at an old well.

With its higgledy-piggledy stone houses and a beautiful seaside setting dominated by the enormous bridges, North Queensferry deserves a potter. Aside from teashops and an upmarket restaurant the town's main attraction is Deep Sea World, one of Britain's best aquariums (particularly if you like sharks). It's also worth wandering out onto the old Town Pier, where ferries used to dock, for a seal's eye perspective on the bridges that replaced them. Now follow the main road up left out of town, bearing right at a fork to reach the landward end of the Forth Road Bridge. Concrete steps lead up onto the walkway at road level; from here it is possible to walk back over the Ferry Hills to Inverkeithing, but better is to continue south over the bridge for the 2km crossing out of Fife. Stay on the left side of the bridge for the best views of its 19th-century predecessor, or on the right side to view its modern replacement, the Queensferry Crossing.

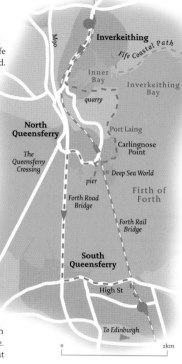

Having crossed out of Fife, make your way down into South Queensferry. The High Street features many fine historic buildings, including Black Castle (built in 1626) and the nearby Tolbooth with its big square tower. Dalmeny train station is a short walk uphill from here.

Humbie Wood and the Heughs

Distance 5.5km **Time** 2 hours **Terrain** farm tracks and woodland paths, some very muddy and others thickly overgrown in summer; above the village you're as likely to see a gliding buzzard as groups of other walkers **Map** OS Explorer 367
Access regular trains to Aberdour from Edinburgh, Dundee and Kirkcaldy; regular buses from Kirkcaldy and Dunfermline

A short but memorable ramble through secretive woods and peaceful hillocks above a historic coastal village.

From Aberdour station, follow the A921 (Main Street) into the eastern half of the village; beyond the corner shop, turn left up Murrell Road. At the top of the road is a long straight path uphill through fields; follow this, with an expanding view of the Forth behind you. Passing a row of sandstone outcrops the track continues into and out of a dip, usually very cattle-churned and muddy. The forested ridge in the background is Cullaloe Wood. Pass a ruined cottage, going straight on between overgrown hedgerows to a gateway between two old trees. Turn right onto a gorse-flanked track, ascending to ruined farm buildings on a low rise, then bear right again to reach the border of Humbie Wood, a secluded island of dense green.

Follow the edge of the wood east and then southeast on a track that climbs to a broad ridge looking towards the Forth Bridges. Here the track turns left and then right, passing gorse-clad hummocks to reach a T-junction, with the day's best view over the island-studded firth to Edinburgh and the rippling Pentland Hills. Go right and then left just before reaching a cottage (going straight on here is a delightful shortcut back to Aberdour), descending

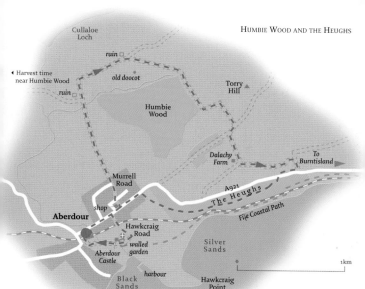

Cullaloe
Loch

ruin

◀ Harvest time
near Humbie Wood

old doocot

ruin

Torry
Hill

Humbie
Wood

Dalachy
Farm

To
Burntisland

Murrell
Road

A921

The Heughs

shop

Aberdour

Fife Coastal Path

Hawkcraig
Road

walled
garden

Silver
Sands

Aberdour
Castle

harbour

Black
Sands

Hawkcraig
Point

0   1km

slightly to Dalachy Farm (if the farmer is in, the best locally-reared beef you'll ever taste is for sale here). Turn left out of the farmyard, following the track downhill past cottages to reach the A921 opposite an impressive little castle.

Turn right, hurrying along the road for about 100 metres (there's no pavement). Look left for the first break in the wall, where a sign for Aberdour and the Coastal Path is concealed. Partially obscured under dense summer undergrowth (trousers useful), a path now descends into The Heughs, an unspoilt strip of coastal woodland. Soon you come to a signposted trail junction; turn right here (the downhill alternative meets the Fife Coastal Path

midway between Aberdour and Burntisland). Now follow the trail westwards with occasional glimpses down through thick foliage to the sea; despite the nearby road this stretch feels very secluded. At one point there's a surprise view over Aberdour's Silver Sands – stunning at sunset. Leaving the sea behind, the path now continues through the woods to rejoin the A921 just east of the village.

Walking back west along Main Street, take the second left down Hawkcraig Road. Cross a railway bridge and turn immediately right through a doorway to reach the train station via the beautiful walled garden of Aberdour Castle.

21

Inchcolm Abbey

Distance 1.5km **Time** allow at least 1 hour 30 ashore if possible **Terrain** rough grassy paths with some steep steps on the eastern headland; the abbey itself is more accessible, though the ferries are not able to accommodate wheelchair users **Map** OS Explorer 367 **Access** in summer there are regular tourist boat departures from South Queensferry's Hawes Pier; in addition to the ferry fare a landing charge is payable on arrival; in the winter there are no public sailings, so you'll have to make your own arrangements. Between late September and late March the Historic Scotland warden is not in residence and the abbey is closed

Take a boat trip to the unforgettable 'Iona of the East', with its cloistered halls, clifftop strolls, seabirds and seals.

A cluster of evocative ruins in a rugged natural setting, Inchcolm Abbey is one of the most interesting historic sites in Scotland. Though close to the mainland, there's a real sense of isolation here; its relative inaccessibility helped protect the abbey from the incursions of Vikings, English and Reformation zealots, and today it remains the best-preserved example of medieval monastic architecture in the country. Inchcolm's Christian heritage dates back to Dark Age hermits, but its holy significance was given the official seal of royal approval rather later, King David I permitting the establishment of an Augustinian priory on the island in 1235. Full abbey status came in the following century. Various extensions were added over the years, and much is still standing. The pillared cloister is practically

◄ Inchcolm Abbey

intact, as are several stairways, roofed halls and even a rare 13th-century fresco.

Inchcolm takes the form of two craggy headlands divided by a low, narrow spit fringed with sandy bays. Boats dock in the northern bay. The abbey is unmissable, and deserves an hour's poking about. Once you've done enough sightseeing, head for the island's western headland, walking out to the furthest tip along grassy paths mown through the rough. Return to the abbey. If there's time it's worth exploring Inchcolm's eastern headland too; to the right of the shop building is a flight of

steps running uphill through scrub, soon reaching the mouth of a brick arched tunnel. This is part of the extensive fortifications built during both World War One and World War Two, when naval batteries protected the strategically vital shipping lanes of the Forth. Walk through the tunnel (which is just long enough to be exciting) to emerge near some crumbling gun emplacements glowering east into the sea. From here a flight of concrete steps leads down to a lower-level path that runs above Inchcolm's sheltered southern bay, returning to the landing area.

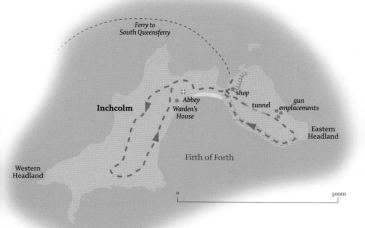

Burntisland and The Binn

Distance 6km **Time** 2 hours 30
Terrain mostly clear, easy tracks, with
steep grassy slopes ascending and
descending The Binn **Map** OS Explorer 367
Access the route is best accessed by train,
starting at Kinghorn railway station and
finishing at Burntisland station; buses
run between Kirkcaldy and Dunfermline
via Kinghorn and Burntisland

A medium-length leg stretcher over a
surprisingly dramatic mini peak, with
some of the most expansive coastal
panoramas in Fife.

From Kinghorn railway station, walk
uphill, then turn left onto Burntisland

Road. Head west towards the edge of town.
Beside the turreted Kinghorn Golf Club
house, turn right onto a track which curves
uphill past another club hut before
crossing the golf course, with a breezy
outlook over the Forth. From a corner
overlooking Pettycur Bay Caravan Park the
track bends away from the sea. At semi-
derelict Grangehill Farm turn left,
continuing west through peaceful rolling
country with a view over Kinghorn Loch to
the distant sweep of Largo Bay. The track
soon begins a gentle descent to meet the
Burntisland to Kinghorn back road (B923).
Turning left, cross the road and take a gated
path on the right, signed for The Binn. This

crosses the site of an old aluminium works, now totally demolished and seemingly returning to nature, then follows the top of a wooded escarpment, quarried in the distant past.

Go straight on towards the tree-covered rise of The Binn, ignoring two left-hand turn-offs, then climbing quite steeply along the margin of a field to reach The Binn's summit ridge; the high point is a little way west. With its crags dropping abruptly into Burntisland and the Forth laid out below, this is a superb vantage point. A panorama plaque indicates the distances to prominent landmarks including the Paps of Fife, the Isle of May, Bass Rock, North Berwick Law, Arthur's Seat, the Pentlands, the Ochils and even (if you're lucky) the Munro Ben Chonzie, nearly 70km away.

Continue west along the ridge with fields on one side and the hill's steep face dropping off on the other. On reaching a knoll at the end of the ridge, the path cuts off rightwards, slightly indistinct at first, to descend a grassy slope leading to a little pond tucked in a fold of the hills. Just left of the pond is a path junction; go left, crossing a field and then descending through woods, passing an old quarry to reach the A909 on the outskirts of Burntisland.

Head into town to reach a roundabout; going straight on, the road curves down to meet the east end of the High Street. Given time and a low tide it's nice to return to Kinghorn across the wide sandy beach (but beware rising water). Alternatively, Burntisland train station is down by the docks to the south of the High Street – it's worth having a poke around the town's historic centre on the way.

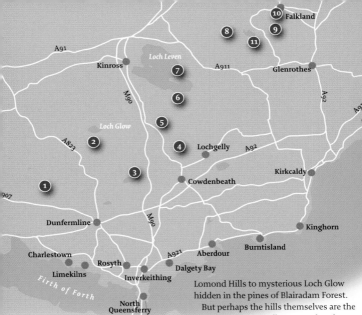

Though close to Fife's major towns, this corner of the Kingdom retains an unspoilt and distinctly rural atmosphere. Woods, hills and water – it's the natural assets that make walking here a real pleasure.

Loch Leven is the loveliest and largest loch in Lowland Scotland and a magnet for teeming birdlife. Though this is officially part of Perth and Kinross, it sits right on urban Fife's doorstep; it's well worth making the cross-border raid to try the new Heritage Trail, which looks set to become a classic walk. With purpose-built paths of its own, wildlife-rich Loch Ore is smaller but similarly attractive. Then there are the hill lochs, from the reservoirs of the

Lomond Hills to mysterious Loch Glow hidden in the pines of Blairadam Forest.

But perhaps the hills themselves are the star attraction – small compared to the Highlands, yet perfectly formed. With their sweeping slopes, crags of volcanic rock and summit views that seem to span the Central Belt, the Lomond Hills have a sense of character and quality out of proportion to their modest scale. Twin-domed summits thrusting pneumatically out of the surrounding countryside, the peaks of West Lomond and East Lomond really suit their local name, the Paps of Fife. Looming steeply over Loch Leven, Benarty and Bishop Hill have plenty of charm too, and are popular for good reason. In contrast, the forested Cleish Hills retain an air of seclusion, and are well worth exploring for a bit of peace and quiet.

East Lomond ▸

Hills and Lochs of the West

Saline Hill and Glen

Distance 6km **Time** 3 hours **Terrain** farm tracks and muddy field paths, then a pathless hill climb on steep grassy slopes and a fairly rough descent; the return leg follows a winding woodland trail **Map** OS Explorer 367 **Access** regular buses from Dunfermline bus station to Saline

Saline Hill combines a relatively quick ascent with some of the best views in Fife – so why is it usually so quiet? The return leg along snaking Saline Glen is an unexpected treat.

From Main Street car park in Saline village centre, cross the road and immediately turn right down Bridge Street past a row of 18th-century stone cottages. By the old cemetery, the road bends left. At Tulohill Cottage, go right onto a farm track, which climbs through fields heading directly towards Saline Hill. At a bend just before Killernie Farm, turn left through a gate, following a faint muddy path along the margin of several fields – a historic right of way. Keep just left of the fenceline, passing through more gates and crossing a burn by a ribbon of Scots pines to join a better-defined track beside a small quarry. Stay on this track briefly along the northern foot of the hill, which is defended by a thick band of gorse.

Where the gorse ends, step over the retaining wall and attack the hillside head on – it is steep, pathless and often cattle-

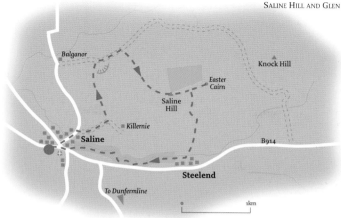

churned. The brutality soon relents as you bear slightly left up a gently sloping shoulder to reach a wall. Follow this for the final steep climb onto Saline Hill's domed summit. The obligatory cairn is just over a wall on top, and from it you can see practically every hill in the Central Belt and even, on a clear day, the Munro peak of Ben Lomond. It is worth continuing east along the edge of a wood for the short, sharp climb onto the neighbouring summit of Easter Cairn, site of a prehistoric fort. The next peak along is Knock Hill. Though it's the highest of the three, multiple antennae on top make it the least attractive to climb. Instead, return to the saddle between Easter Cairn and Saline Hill, then head south to descend towards the village of Steelend. It's steep and there's no path, but the angle rapidly eases. Once down on more level ground, walk along right along a fenceline

to find a gate. Still heading directly for Steelend, descend a rough slope, climb a fence on an earth bank and cross a grassy field to reach the edge of the village.

Hop across another low fence and a narrow burn to pick up a path on the far bank. Follow this west through a little park at the back of the houses. At the far corner of the park the path dips into the trees of Saline Glen, a ribbon of ancient woodland sheltered in a steep-sided ravine. Pass some overgrown cliffs and ignore a stile on the left, staying with the glen path as it follows the winding course of the burn downstream. It's muddy in places, but beautiful. Steps lead under an aqueduct, and the path then crosses and re-crosses the burn on wooden footbridges before passing a terraced garden on the right. The trail eventually emerges in the middle of Saline, where you'll want to go and do it all again.

Dumglow and Loch Glow

Distance 7km Time 3 hours
Terrain stretches on tarmac and gravel
tracks, but elsewhere faint and boggy
paths with some short, sharp ascents and
plenty of rough ground; map and compass
useful in low cloud, while gaiters might
prove welcome in wet weather
Map OS Explorer 367 Access no public
transport to the start of this route; a
longer day might start with a bus to Kelty
and an approach to the described walk via
Blairadam Forest (see page 32)

With its lonely lochs and surprising rocky
summits, this is one of the most varied
hill walks in Fife, and rarely busy.

Drive along the minor road over the
Cleish Hills to park in a lay-by at the
mouth of a forest track (GR100955), popular
with anglers and dog walkers. From the
forestry gate the track runs into the woods
between impenetrable walls of pine,
passing a turn-off, curving right and then
meeting the shore of Loch Glow at its little
dam. The scale of this secluded hill loch
may come as a surprise; the forest-fringed
humps of Dumglow and The Inneans
reflect in the water, and silence reigns. Take
a path along the south shore – quite wet in
places – bearing right around the far end of
the loch and hopping the bogs (plank
bridges span the worst bits) to reach a
drystone wall. Walk parallel to this,
heading roughly WNW over waterlogged
open ground.

Pass just left of Black Loch in a hollow
overlooked by Dumglow's broken
rocks, bearing north around the far end of

◄ Dumglow from Loch Glow

the water and climbing a rough pathless slope towards the saddle just west of Dumglow. Climb a fence via a stone stile, then attack the left flank of the summit hump – steep, rough and practically pathless. The view from the concrete trig point on top takes in a wide swathe of country including the Fife, Lothian and Ochil hills, and the Wallace Monument above Stirling.

Descend east on a faint path through grassy hummocks to meet the forest boundary at a wooden stile. Beyond this, the path plunges into a gloomy conifer tunnel, heading downhill to cross a fenceline in a firebreak. Keep heading straight on (almost due east), now along a

better-defined break, with the middle peak of the three Inneans dead ahead, passing a broad track junction to reach open ground again. A short, sharp pull gains the central summit. Looking north, the lower, rockier peak of Dummiefarline can be seen, standing just outside the woods; though there's a quick return direct from The Inneans to Loch Glow, it is worth making a detour over rolling grassy slopes to climb this outlier. From Dummiefarline's summit cairn descend roughly east on a faint path, passing just left of Lurg Loch to rejoin the Cleish road about 10 minutes' walk from the car park.

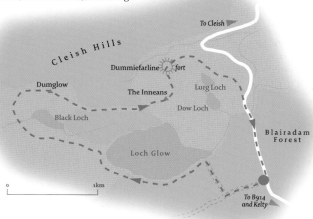

Mines of Blairadam Forest

Distance 4km **Time** 2 hours **Terrain** well-graded forest tracks and paths – should be passable with an all-terrain buggy **Map** OS Explorer 367 **Access** Kelty is about 1.5km away; access to the forest is more convenient by car (from junction 4 on the M90 head west on the B914; take the first right, turning into the woods at a Forestry Commission sign; follow the track to the public car park beside the forestry depot)

A mellow meander through deep woods, with some industrial heritage and an unexpected finish along a hidden glen.

The pre-eminent architect of his day, William Adam purchased this area in 1733, building the grand house from which Blairadam Forest gets its name. Adam sired an illustrious line of architects, his sons John, Robert and James all following in his footsteps. Robert, in particular, is widely considered to be the most influential neo-classicist of the late 18th century. As well as designing great buildings, the family were no slouches on the business front. Initially there were few trees on the estate, so Adam Senior started planting both for ornamentation and commercial timber, a process now continued by the Forestry Commission. The family also developed an interest in coal mining. This age-old local activity really took off in the 19th century; at its

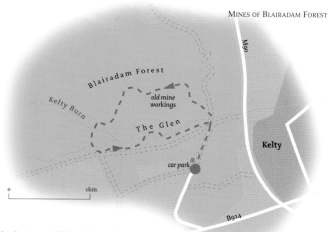

Blairadam Forest

Kelty Burn

old mine workings

The Glen

Kelty

M90

car park

B914

0   1km

height the town of Kelty had ten pits. Traces of mining activity can still be seen among the pines.

There are several marked trails in the woods; this walk uses the best bits of two. In addition to these, there are many other side paths weaving into the trees for you to explore, popular with mountain bikers.

From the car park beside the forestry depot, start by following the yellow waymarks on a track running slightly downhill past a totem pole and a frieze carved into a brick wall. At a major junction take the second left, a wide gravel track that crosses Kelty Burn, passing a small tree-covered crag. After 500m turn left again to reach the spoil heaps of an old mine, now being reclaimed by the woods. Beyond the mine a well-laid walking path curves through a stand of young oaks, then wiggles gradually uphill, where more deciduous groves provide a welcome contrast to the impenetrable pine.

At a junction the route kinks sharply left over a small burn, then crosses an arched stone bridge spanning a second burn. Soon after, branch left to enter The Glen, descending past the confluence of the two burns and going with the flow downstream. You're now no longer following yellow markers, so look out instead for the red ones. The path stays close to the rushing burn as it wiggles through a secluded mini valley cloaked in mature pines and bird-friendly thickets. You may see deer in the woods, or hear the mewling call of buzzards gliding above the canopy. Pass the collapsed brick piers of an old mine-access railway bridge – though there's not much to see nowadays. Cross and re-cross the burn to rejoin the original forest track not far short of the big junction that you first came to; turn right and soon regain the car park.

◀ Crag in Blairadam Forest

33

Lochore Meadows Country Park

Distance 6km **Time** 1 hour 30
Terrain level pushchair-friendly paths
with an optional slightly rougher
variation along the south shore of the
loch **Map** OS Explorer 367 – the route
inconveniently spans both sides of the
sheet, but a map isn't really needed
– just follow the blue waymarkers
Access buses run from Rosyth to Ballingry
via Dunfermline and Cowdenbeath; alight
at Crosshill; bus from Glenrothes to
Dunfermline stops at Crosshill too

A quick, easy circuit around an attractive
bird-rich loch, regenerated after decades
of heavy industry.

Though a wildlife haven, Lochore
Meadows Country Park is actually an
artificial landscape. This part of Fife has a
proud coal mining heritage dating back

many centuries. Mining was the lifeblood
of Ballingry and surrounding villages
through the Industrial Revolution, but pit
closures in the 1950s and '60s left a
wasteland of derelict collieries, slurry
ponds and spoil heaps. Over several
decades the mess was cleared, topsoil laid,
a new loch created and more than one
million trees planted. These woods are
now managed to be as biodiverse as
possible. The huge Mary Pit winding gear
is one of the only remaining monuments
to Lochore's underground past; today's
country park is a healthy environment for
wildlife and outdoor recreation.

There are several waymarked walking
trails in the park; the longest is the round-
the-loch route, marked by occasional blue
squiggles. From the sandy beach by the
park centre car park, bear right along the

◄ Reeds of Loch Ore

north shore of Loch Ore on a level gravel track. Pushy swans might try to mug you for your lunch here. Having passed wooded Tod Island the shore is soon obscured by reeds and scrub, good cover for water birds. Turn left onto a tarmac drive, passing a turn-off for Harran Hill Woods (worth a detour in spring). At the next junction go left again, through a gate into the nature reserve. Follow a long straight stretch with extensive wetlands on the right (Loch Ore itself is hidden in trees on the left) to reach a footbridge over the sluggish burn that drains the loch.

Beyond is a T-junction. A short walk west is a birdwatching hide beside a small pond, another worthwhile detour – the park teems with over-wintering ducks, and there are many summer visitors too.

The round-the-loch path heads east, soon meeting the open loch shore with a view up to Benarty Hill. There's now a choice of trail, a pushchair-friendly 'inland' track or the muddier but more interesting waterside path.

Passing two reed-fringed islands, continue east through rocky knolls, with some rough ground underfoot if you've taken the shore path. The two routes soon rejoin for the final leg. Beyond some houses, turn left, crossing a bridged weir over the loch's outflow and passing an outdoor education centre to return to the park centre.

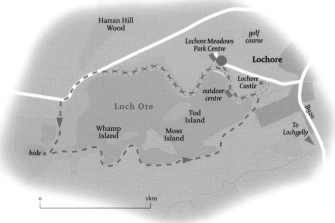

A blast up Benarty Hill

Distance 4km **Time** 2 hours
Terrain narrow hill paths with some steep
ascents and descents, and rough ground
on the summit ridge **Map** OS Explorer 367
– the route cuts across both sides of the
map; the ascent path is not marked
Access regular buses from Dunfermline,
Glenrothes and Kirkcaldy to
Lochore/Ballingry, followed by a fairly
short walk through Lochore Meadows
Country Park (*see page* 34) or along the road
at the bottom of Benarty Hill

**A short, sharp ascent on a rugged mini
mountain with extensive loch and
country panoramas – a good introduction
to hillwalking.**

Craggy Benarty looks great from the
M90 motorway, but the best route up it is
on the hill's quieter southern flank.
A track runs from the Lochore Meadows
Country Park centre to meet the minor
road along the southern base of Benarty
Hill (GR159969). Either use the limited
roadside car parking here or walk from the
country park (the latter option adds some
distance to the day). From the minor road
a wooden-stepped path signed for Benarty
winds steeply uphill into the woods, with
an expanding view of the distant Lothian
skyline to the south. Turn left onto a
forestry track at a T-junction; the track
soon becomes a grassy path, wiggling
through the pines to reach the forest edge.

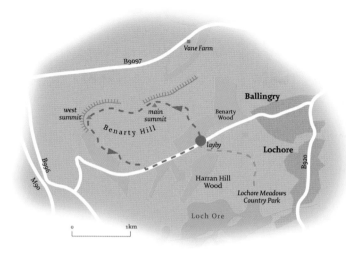

Hop over the low fence and take a path through heathery moorland, which follows the wood's edge briefly before peeling leftwards to make a gradual ascent over hummocky ground to reach the trig point on Benarty's main summit. This gives a sudden panorama across Loch Leven to the Lomond Hills.

Head west, following a wall and fence along the broad ridge top, the official border between Fife and Kinross-shire. Just to the right are some impressive cliffs overlooking Loch Leven, though they're hard to spot from above. Beyond a little dip is a short, sharp ascent onto a slightly lower summit, site of a prehistoric hillfort. Now for a quick border raid into Kinross-

shire. Climb over another low wall and continue along the ridge crest, with rough ground underfoot, to reach the far west summit, a perch looking over the M90 to the Cleish Hills and the Ochils.

Continue SSE along the edge of the steep craggy slope. Frequent signposts warn of a rifle range on the slopes below, and when a red flag is flying it's wise to stay left of them. Keeping left of a wood, follow an electric fence line to a gate in a field corner. Pass a telecom mast to meet a grassy track. This curves briefly left, then descends gently southeast through fields, quite indistinct in places, to meet the road at a locked gate. Turn left, returning to the start point in approximately 1km.

Two views of Vane Farm

Distance 3km Time 2 hours Terrain well-graded signed trails throughout, with some fairly steep ascents and descents; pushchair pushers would enjoy the Wetland Trail, but not the Woodland Walk; as this is a nature reserve please stick to the paths and respect the locals
Map OS Explorer 369 Access very limited bus connections to Kinross

Marked trails through a showpiece RSPB reserve; the low-lying wetland leg offers fantastic birdwatching possibilities, while the optional hill climb offers memorable views over Loch Leven.

Vane Farm is a major RSPB reserve in a beautiful loch shore location. With its mix of wetlands and wooded hillside, it swarms with a rich variety of birdlife; there is an excellent visitor centre and a cosy café too, with viewing windows overlooking Loch Leven and a collection of telescopes that are free to use. Families are welcome and wildlife-spotting packs provided for children. The modest entry fee goes towards protecting this precious environment, but if you really want to help then consider joining the RSPB while you're here.

From the shop, go left through a pedestrian tunnel under the B9097. Follow a sign for the Wetland Trail downhill past a meadow, the world's first bumblebee sanctuary, to a large viewing hide. Turn left along a banked path, sown with wildflowers and buzzing with insects in summer, to a T-junction. There's a hide at each end of the T, both providing close-up

◀ Bishop Hill from Vane Farm

views of the many waders, ducks and geese. Return uphill to the visitor centre.

Now for the optional hill climb. From outside the café and shop entrance, follow the signed Woodland Walk. Go through a picnic area and head left along the Viewpoint Loop, a well-graded path that winds uphill through thriving birchwoods. Look out for nesting boxes up in the trees. After a decent climb, branch left at a path junction, still following the Viewpoint Loop. The woods soon thin out as you reach the brow of the hill at a cairn and benches, with inspiring views across Loch Leven to the Lomond and Ochil hills;

there's even a glimpse of that other great bird sanctuary, Bass Rock, in the mouth of the Forth.

Stay on the path heading roughly south through the heather, soon descending back into birchwoods. Turn left at a junction, beyond which footbridges cross three little burns in a row. The path then descends fairly steeply before looping back rightwards to re-cross the burns at a lower level. Now fairly level, the path leads along the bottom of the woods and back through the picnic area to reach the visitor centre again. It would be a shame to miss out on the welcoming café while you're here.

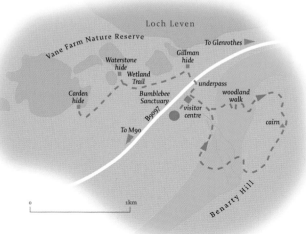

Loch Leven Heritage Trail

**Distance 19.5km Time 6 hours
Terrain** a well-engineered gravel-surfaced
trail throughout – bicycle, pushchair and
wheelchair friendly **Map** OS Explorer 369
Access bus to Kinross. If you are walking
only a section of the whole trail then
you'll either need to return to your
starting point by bus, arrange to leave a
car at either end of your route, or retrace
your steps. Bus services can be limited,
especially at weekends

A recently established route and already
a classic, this long but gentle lochside
trail leads through the woods and
wetlands surrounding Loch Leven –
twitcher heaven.

Scotland's largest lowland loch is a
wildlife-rich shallow lagoon in a
picturesque bowl of farmland ringed by
craggy little hills. This National Nature
Reserve is internationally important for
breeding and migrating waterfowl,
including ducks, geese and assorted
waders; over 20,000 pink-footed geese
visit in autumn, nearly 10% of the entire
world population. Since the initial
opening of the Loch Leven Heritage Trail
in 2008, and its completion several years
later, the loch has become the ideal
habitat for walkers too. With its mix of
shoreline, woods and fields this all-day
circuit has become hugely popular among
weekend strollers and cyclists alike, and
must surely be among the best low-level
trails in Central Scotland. If the whole
route seems a bit much it's possible to
break it down into shorter sections.

From the angling centre in Kinross go
left to follow the Heritage Trail along the

Milnathort

A911

Burleigh
Sands

Kinross

Kinross
House

Castle Island
Lochleven Castle

pier   ferry

Loch Leven

St Serf's Island

Levenmouth
Woods

RSPB
Loch Leven

Vane Farm

B9097   Benarty Hill

B996

0   2km

loch shore through Kirkgate Park. Trace the outer boundary of the grounds of Kinross House, staying mostly in woods with only an occasional glimpse of the nearby water. Soon pass a turn-off to a bird watching hide – it's worth a look, both for the birds and the views over the reed-fringed loch to the Lomond Hills. Easy walking takes you alongside golf courses, across a footbridge over a small burn and past a couple more wildlife hides to Burleigh Sands. With its shallow beach backed by mature Scots pines this is perhaps the most idyllic stretch of the Heritage Trail.

Beyond an old ruined church the path peels away from the loch shore, passing through open farmland and then a stretch of woods. Now close to the loch's east shore the route follows the top of a long earth embankment, with views up to nearby Kinnesswood and Bishop Hill. As you near Loch Leven's southeast corner the trail winds through pretty Levenmouth Woods, eventually crossing a bridge over the River Leven. Heading back west, the riverbank is followed to an old sluice house at the loch's outflow. Beyond is a little sandy bay, and a stretch along

the shore below Vane Hill to the Vane Farm RSPB reserve, where there's a welcoming café and various nature trails (see page 38).

Continuing west the trail shadows the B9097 for a while, with a wide open outlook to compensate for the road noise. Look out for wading birds in the adjacent reserve (binoculars help). On a slight rise sits the East Brackley Viewpoint, a swish wooden shelter with some lovely stone sculptures. From here the trail turns away from the road, running downhill to the loch shore. With superb views over the water, a final long stretch now leads back to Kinross.

◄ Lomond Hills over Loch Leven

West Lomond via Glen Vale

Distance 7km **Time** 3 hours 30
Terrain clear path and road walking
contrasts with sections on which the trail
is far from obvious, and the ground very
uneven and steep **Map** OS Explorer 370
Access the nearest bus stops are at Wester
Balgedie on the A911 and Gateside on the
A91 – both options add a little extra road
walking to the day

A superb strenuous hill walk on Fife's
highest summit, with rough ground, weird
rock formations and sweeping views.

From the car park and picnic area
(GR172070) take the single-track road
southwest, turning left onto a woodland
footpath at a sign for Glen Vale. The path
soon crosses a footbridge, leaving the
trees to follow Glen Burn upstream,
staying on open ground on the north
side of the narrow burn cutting. The going
can be muddy. Entering Glen Vale, the
tight cleft between West Lomond and
Bishop Hill, the route passes beneath
the bulging sandstone outcrop of John
Knox's Pulpit, where clandestine sermons
were held during the Reformation. In a
fit of health and safety hysteria, Fife
Council demolished half of it in 2004.
Ascend left of a waterfall in a deep gorge,
above which the glen opens into a broad
heathery trough.

On reaching a rutted track, turn hard left,
tracing a faint and easily-lost path

To Strathmiglo

Bonnet Stane

Craigen Gaw

To Maspie Den and Falkland

Glen Burn

West Lomond

Miller's Loch

Edge Head

John Knox's Pulpit

Devil's Burdens

Glen Vale

0   1km

northwards up a long tussocky incline. Another route in this book (*see page 48*) stays on this course up West Lomond, but for an alternative ascent curve left to follow a slight ridge running along the top of a row of rocks, the Devil's Burdens, then bear north again to reach the shoulder called Wind and Weather (often appropriate). Cross a low wall, heading east to pick up a well-used path for the final steep ascent to West Lomond's summit cairn and trig point. Go down at first the way you came up, but stay with the path a little longer in descent as it begins to curve rightwards around the base of the summit cone. Soon quit it, branching off northwest to meet the edge of the dramatic steep escarpment that is a particular characteristic of the Lomond Hills.

Though it can be hard to spot from above (especially if the clouds are low), a rough path descends steeply, cutting almost due west at first down a shallow grassy scoop in the slope to pass beneath a layer of broken rocks (these aren't a sensible descent alternative). Crossing a stile, the route then follows a fenceline before slanting down across a grassy field to reach the weird mushroom-shaped sandstone pinnacle of the Bonnet Stane. The Maiden Bower, a carved chamber at the base of the rocks, is a good place for a sheltered breather. From here, head roughly north to make a gradual descent along field boundaries back to the single-track road at a different car park. Turning left, a 15-minute road walk brings you back to the starting point.

◀ West Lomond from the north

East Lomond via Maspie Den

Distance 6km **Time** 2 hours 30
Terrain clear paths all the way, but
with some steep sections around the
summit cone **Map** OS Explorer 370
Access regular Glenrothes to Perth buses
stop at Falkland

**An historic village, a hidden glen with
unexpected surprises, deep woods and
one of the most iconic peaks in Fife – it's
a short walk, but a fantastic one.**

From the centre of Falkland, go up the
West Port and continue to the end of the
public road in the Falkland Estate (parking
here). Pass the arched stable block and
follow the tarmac drive through the trees,
branching right to avoid the entrance to
Falkland House School. At a little bridge is
a signed path for Maspie Den; take this,
skirting the school grounds and following
the burn uphill through dark woods. Go
under an arched bridge and then through

a curved stone tunnel (kids will love it),
then a wooden footway under another
stone arch. The path wiggles up the
ravine under tall pines, crossing various
footbridges and passing several cascades.
Suddenly you come to one of the most
unusual features seen on any walk in
Fife, a carved rock gallery running behind
a waterfall. Once you've had your fun
with this, continue up stone steps on
the left to a viewpoint looking back down
the Den and up to the distinctive conical
peak of East Lomond. It's easy to see why
the twin Lomonds are affectionately
known as the Paps.

Go left at the next junction, then right
through a gate in a deer fence, beyond
which the path runs parallel to the single-
track Falkland to Glenrothes road,
climbing steadily through a swathe of
felled forestry for just over 1km. Go
through another gate into a patch of pine,

◀ Maspie Den

the path now leading to a car park and picnic area at the road's high point. Opposite is a path signed for East Lomond.

This ascends gradually over breezy open ground, making straight for East Lomond, with an extensive outlook north to the eastern Ochils and south to the Firth of Forth. At a signpost go left through a gate, the path continuing quite gently before a cruel sting in the tail, a leg-sapping slog up the abrupt summit cone. Extensive earthworks here are the remains of a prehistoric hillfort, an easily defended site with views to kill for. A modern panorama display shows all the distant landmarks that you can't see on a cloudy day; Dundee's tower blocks, the high

Cairngorms, the Trossachs, Arthur's Seat and Bass Rock in the mouth of the Forth. Descend ENE on a rough path – again it's very steep at first, although the angle soon relents. With Falkland now directly below, go over a stile and soon re-enter forestry. A long flight of slippery wooden steps leads down through the trees. Go right at a T-junction, and then right again a while later on a track that leads into Falkland by the bag factory (you can't miss it). Walk into the village centre for a well-earned pot of tea or a pint.

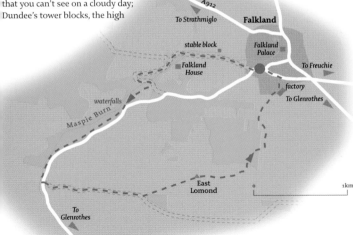

Royal Falkland

Distance 5km **Time** 3 hours 30 (if you're doing the palace justice) **Terrain** the village streets and palace gardens couldn't be easier, but the optional extension through the Falkland Estate makes use of stony forest tracks and muddy paths with some fairly steep ascents and descents **Map** OS Explorer 370 **Access** regular Glenrothes to Perth buses stop at Falkland

Explore one of the finest ancient buildings in Scotland and the beautiful village at its gates, followed by an optional woodland leg to an unusual monument.

From Back Wynd car park, head down Horse Market and turn right along

the High Street, or simply wander at random through the quiet streets and narrow wynds in the pretty heart of Falkland, a remarkably well-preserved village with a long and fascinating history. Take time to read the inscriptions on the walls and lintels of the old townhouses and weavers' cottages. As you'd expect from Fife's most visitor-friendly village, there are plenty of restaurants, tearooms and welcoming pubs; antique fans shouldn't miss the violin shop.

The impressive 16th-century edifice of Falkland Palace dominates the north side of the village. Originally a simple castle, it was massively extended and improved by

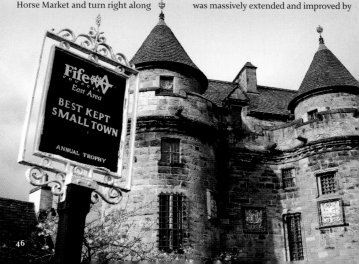

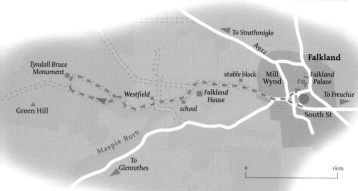

James IV and V to create a holiday home fit for the pickiest monarch. Generations of royalty stayed here when touring the country or visiting to hunt in the nearby forest. Having fallen into disrepair, it was partially restored in the 19th century, and remains a superb example of French-flavoured Renaissance architecture.

Though it is still owned by the bearer of the hereditary title Keeper of Falkland Palace, a large part of the building is on show to the public thanks to the National Trust for Scotland; it's well worth paying the entry fee. Lavishly furnished apartments, original Stewart décor, the stunning Chapel Royal, extensive well-kept grounds and the oldest surviving 'real' tennis court in the world – if you've ever wondered how the upper crust used to live this is a real eye opener.

Having 'done' the village and palace, more energetic walkers might fancy something completely different. Head west along the High Street and then West Port

to enter Falkland Estate. Beyond a duck pond and an old stable block, bear left through trees a little way above Maspie Burn (ignore the path closer to the water) to pass Falkland House School. Stay left on the track to pass by some houses, then go straight on at the next fork, climbing steeply to enter thick pine woods. The track splits again: stay left, zigzagging up a hill. After a few hundred metres, the gradient levels out; a very faint path on the right then leads through pines to the impressive tower of the Tyndall Bruce Monument, with a commanding view over the flat lands below. If you're not sure footed, it's best to return the way you came. Otherwise, go northeast to descend the steep slope on a slippery scrappy path and pick up a slightly better contouring trail. Turn right along this to return to the forest track used in your ascent.

Lomond Hills grand tour

Distance 19km Time 6 hours Terrain clear paths and tracks, except for one section where the trail is easily lost; some rough and boggy ground with occasional very steep ascents and descents; competent navigation is needed in poor weather Map OS Explorer 370 Access easiest by car; bus users can travel from Glenrothes to Leslie, making a 2.5km walk to the start of the route as described

The classic hillwalking horseshoe of the area, linking all three of the Lomond Hills in one long hard day.

From the parking lay-by beside Holl Reservoir, walk back down the road towards the pylons, then turn right onto a long straight track signed for Bishop Hill. This rises steadily to pass West Feal Farm, then follows the edge of a forestry plantation on Munduff Hill before briefly entering the woods. At the far edge of the

forest, continue straight ahead on a muddy track through hummocky country to reach the edge of Bishop Hill's steep western escarpment, looking out over Loch Leven to the distant green ridge of the Ochils. The path now curves right. Ignore a downhill turn-off, and make your way to Bishop Hill's cairned summit, the highest of several hummocks.

A short, steep descent and a leg over bumpy ground brings you to a wall that cuts across the ridge. Head right along this, with the distinctive form of East Lomond dead ahead, to descend boggy slopes past a scattering of old pine. At a gate turn left along another wall, now heading towards the tent-shaped dome of West Lomond, to enter the broad expanse of upper Glen Vale. Join a track briefly, turning off at the first bend onto a vague path for the rough, relentlessly steep climb towards the distant summit of West Lomond. The

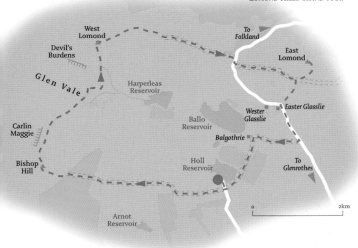

muddy path braids into several strands, and though it's easily lost the general idea is simply to keep going up (*a more circuitous but less calf-busting alternative is described on page 42*). The summit cairn is met with relief – eventually.

A very steep grassy path drops roughly ENE, curving leftwards to a junction down on the plateau beneath West Lomond's summit bulge. Now follow a wide track more or less east on a long gradual descent to meet the minor road that runs over the Lomond Hills from Glenrothes to Falkland. From outside the car park, take a path signed for East Lomond (*as for route on page 44*). This rises gently across open ground to reach a track junction. Here, go left through a gate, beyond which the path climbs gradually before a very steep final sprint up

East Lomond's summit cone. Most of Fife is visible from here, as well as the Lothian hills and a swathe of the distant Highlands.

Descend the way you came to the track junction, then head south on a path signed Limekilns Trail. Branch right past the old kiln, crossing a footbridge and a stile to leave the works behind. Climb a ladder stile over a drystone wall, then continue roughly south across a field – a tall marker pole shows the way – to regain the minor road at a corner by Easter Glasslie Farm. Take the road downhill for approximately 1km, then turn off right onto a farm track. This leads along a vague ridge to reach a house at Balgothrie; turn left here, where a path leads over a low rise and through a forestry plantation to meet the Holl Reservoir dam.

◄ On East Lomond above Falkland

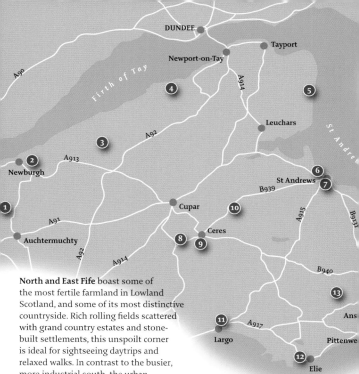

DUNDEE

Tayport

Newport-on-Tay

4

5

A90

Firth of Tay

A914

Leuchars

A92

3

St Andre

2

A913

Newburgh

6

St Andrews

7

1

B939

Cupar

10

A915

A91

8

Ceres

B931

Auchtermuchty

9

A92

A914

B940

North and East Fife boast some of the most fertile farmland in Lowland Scotland, and some of its most distinctive countryside. Rich rolling fields scattered with grand country estates and stone-built settlements, this unspoilt corner is ideal for sightseeing daytrips and relaxed walks. In contrast to the busier, more industrial south, the urban centres here are small and genteel, as exemplified by the handsome market town of Cupar and venerable St Andrews, one of the most attractive and interesting towns in Scotland.

Routes in this part of the Kingdom range from the easiest of strolls through the well-kept gardens and grounds of historic buildings to short, scenic climbs among the little known summits and secretive folds of the eastern Ochils, a tranquil and

13

Ans

11

A917

Pittenwe

Largo

12

Elie

unspoilt range of hills that few walkers seem to be aware of. There are woodland hikes in dense forests and snaking gorge-like dens, days out exploring ancient towns and villages, and coastal routes in diverse settings from the sheltered mudflats of the Tay Estuary to the wide golden sands of Tentsmuir and St Andrews. And on the rocks of Kincraig Point is the famous Elie Chain Walk, Fife's ultimate adventure route.

On the beach at Elie

North Fife and the East Neuk

A917

Crail

Pitmedden Forest pathways

Distance 8km **Time** 3 hours **Terrain** a mix of wide forest tracks and narrow muddy paths with many tree roots; one rough descent on which the trail is hard to follow; watch out for flying mountain bikers **Map** OS Explorer 370 **Access** bus travellers can get as far as Auchtermuchty; from there, it's a 1.5km uphill road walk to the start of the route as described

Pleasant forest walking on the low wooded ridge of the eastern Ochils, rising between the interesting old villages of Abernethy and Auchtermuchty.

To get to the Forestry Commission car park, take the Newburgh road from Auchtermuchty, branching left just before leaving town on a minor road which climbs to meet the trees; park at the signed lay-by on the right. Pitmedden Forest is very popular with mountain bikers, and a maze of bike trails winds through the pines; to avoid getting lost follow the route instructions closely. Start on a path running along the edge of the wood just next to the road. Ignoring any turn-offs, climb over a low rise and descend to a path junction beside a burn. Follow this upstream to meet the road again at Newhill Farm. Branch right when the road forks, then as the tarmac road becomes a muddy forest track re-enter the woods at a Forestry Commission sign. Turn left onto an earthy path that runs parallel to the forest track, and when this splits stay left to rejoin the track once more.

Keep with the obvious broad main track, going straight on past several turn-offs. At a picnic table by a big old tree, there's a view to the wooded ridge you'll be walking

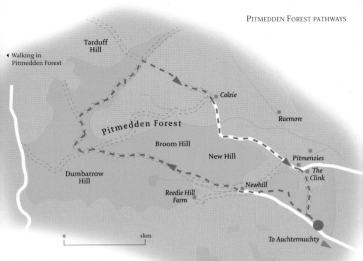

along in a while. The track now winds gently through a more open area of younger planting. Ignore a path on the right by some boulders, staying with the main track to pass a boggy hollow on the left. At the next major junction, turn right onto a gated track that follows the crest of the hill, winding through an attractive landscape of Scots pines and hummocks, with occasional glimpses through the trees to the surrounding countryside. Passing many mountain bikers' side routes, the track swings hard left, then curves back right beside a group of little ponds. A while later it briefly emerges from the pines at the southern edge of the forest before dipping back into the trees. Now keep your eyes peeled for a faint mossy path on the right, which arrives very rapidly – just before a cyclists' waymarker post on the main track.

Follow this rough path out of the woods, soon crossing a stile. The tussocky trail is easily lost among a labyrinth of gorse bushes; stay well right of a marshy burn, making directly for the houses at Colzie. Crossing a fence and a grassy field, pick up a farm track that leads around a gorse-covered knoll to reach the houses. Turn right through the farmyard, then follow the drive downhill to meet a tarmac road at some stables. The road leads along a forest edge, descending past Pitmenzies to cross a burn. Take the second turn-off on the right, passing a caravan park at The Clink to follow a muddy track back through the woods and regain the Auchtermuchty road; the car park is a short way left.

53

Newburgh and Ormiston Hill

Distance 5km **Time** 2 hours 30
Terrain a confusion of trails on Ormiston
Hill, sometimes steep and muddy; the
riverside path along the Tay is much
gentler **Map** OS Explorer 370 **Access** Perth
to Glenrothes buses stop at Newburgh

**A scenic hill climb above a sleepy
Georgian town, with an optional return
along the banks of the Tay; either leg
could be done separately for a shorter day.**

From the west end of the main street,
turn left on Woodriffe Road, signed for
Ninewells Farm B&B, going uphill over a
railway bridge. Beyond a bend, branch left
up a steep, straight side road to pass a
housing estate. At a crossroads beside a
playground, turn left along a muddy track,
through a gate and into a field. A faint path
cuts diagonally up across the grass to a
break in the field boundary near a little
ruined brick structure. Turn right at a path
junction. The trail wiggles up to a wooden

swing gate; turn right again. The well-
established (though often muddy) path
now curves steeply uphill through dense
thickets to emerge at an open area. Head
straight on uphill to reach the grassy
saddle between the three distinct summit
knolls of Ormiston Hill.

The highest point is the gorse-fringed
hummock on the right, site of an ancient
hill fort. Locating the rough path to the
huge summit cairn requires some fence
climbing and prickly probing, but it's
worth the effort for the view over the
silvery Tay and the wrinkled folds of the
eastern Ochils. Returning to the grassy
saddle, backtrack very briefly and then
climb onto the hummock that overlooks
Newburgh. A rough muddy path follows a
fenceline along the gorse-cloaked ridge
before descending under powerlines. Bear
left to contour the hillside parallel to a
lower power line, then take a mucky track
slightly uphill to skirt around a huge

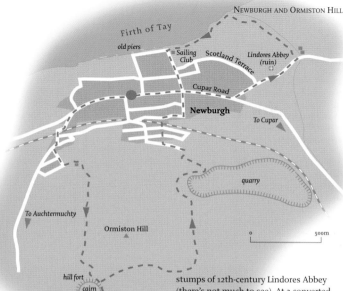

working quarry (this has expanded since OS maps were last updated). Stay with the quarry perimeter fence to descend to a T-junction. The right fork leads to a grassy hillock overlooking Newburgh, with benches and an information board. The left branch descends, passing through a swing gate and into town.

Cut down steps on the right, taking a narrow wynd between houses and over a railway footbridge. Turn right past a turreted stone house and follow the back road down to the east end of the main street. For the optional riverside extension turn right, past a school, and then left along Abbey Road to reach the ivy-covered stumps of 12th-century Lindores Abbey (there's not much to see). At a converted steading, turn left onto a burn-side footpath, following the reed-fringed bank across low lying ground to meet the shore of the Tay itself. Walk along the grassy dyke to re-enter town at Newburgh Sailing Club. Look back east from here to see an enormous figure carved in a distant hillside. This bear and ragged staff is a heraldic device of the earls of Warwick, dating back to Lindores' first Norman abbot (though the hill carving is much more recent).

Turn left past Newburgh FC to return to the main street, with its terraces of solid Georgian houses that attest to the time when this quiet town was a bustling fishing port.

◄ Newburgh on the Tay

Norman's Law

Distance 6km **Time** 2 hours **Terrain** farm
tracks and rough paths with a steep
ascent and descent; it may be a quick
route, but it is best suited to fitter walkers
Map OS Explorer 370 **Access** Luthrie is a
short bus ride from Cupar

**A brief hill walk in the rolling eastern
Ochils – it's not often that such extensive
summit panoramas are won with so
little effort.**

This is the highest peak in the Ochils
east of the M90, and though that's not
really saying much, Norman's Law is still a
surprisingly impressive little hill and one

of the most notable viewpoints in
Southern Scotland. A farm track heads
west from the tiny village of Luthrie,
signed for Norman's Law. Follow the long
straight track, then go right at a junction
by a cottage. The track bends left past a
house before rising gradually along the
border of a wood. At a junction by another
house, follow a signpost pointing right,
staying with the curving track to climb
among wooded knolls. At a fork keep left,
going uphill through a gate and across
rough open ground onto a saddle between
two mini peaks, where the rounded
summit cone of Norman's Law is visible

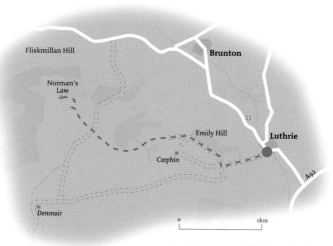

Fliskmillan Hill

Brunton

Norman's
Law

Emily Hill

Luthrie

Carphin

A92

Denmuir

0   1km

for the first time. Break slightly right on a sketchy path, skirting below the rocky knoll on the right and making straight for Norman's Law.

The path cuts between two groups of pines, then crosses a stile and bisects a track, heading straight on to climb quite steeply around the left flank of a rough heathery shoulder. Slog up the final grassy lump onto the summit of Norman's Law itself, which is marked by a large cairn, a trig point and a panorama plaque pointing out the distance and direction of the most prominent landmarks to be seen. These are many and varied, including Arthur's Seat and the Pentlands above Edinburgh, the Lomonds, the Sidlaws above Dundee's tower block skyline and the much higher

peaks of the western Ochils. On a clear day, especially in a snowy winter, an array of high peaks are visible, from the Trossachs, Ben Lawers and Schiehallion to Beinn a'Ghlo and Lochnagar.

Being such a prominent and defensible summit, Norman's Law is inevitably the site of a prehistoric hillfort, and the extensive ramparts can be easily discerned. For those wanting a longer walk, two circuits are possible from here: one option goes north along the track at the hill's foot to meet a tiny public road which winds back rightwards to Luthrie; the other heads south along this same track to pick up a farm road running from Denmuir to Luthrie. However, neither option is as attractive as the way you climbed the hill, so this is one of those rare occasions when it's best to retrace your steps.

◂ Norman's Law from the east

Balmerino loop

Distance 14km Time 4 hours Terrain clear
paths and farm tracks; a couple of the
footbridges in Birkhill Woods are in
disrepair and need to be crossed with
care **Map OS Explorer 371 Access** travel to
Wormit via Newport-on-Tay or Dundee;
from here a local bus connects with
Balmerino

**The best and longest coastal woodland
walk in Fife, with superb views of Dundee
and the Firth of Tay and a chance to spot
red squirrels.**

From the car park at the far end of Bay
Road follow the Fife Coastal Path west
along the shore, signed for Balmerino,
with a good view of the Tay Rail Bridge and
the bird-teeming mudflats at low tide. This
soon cuts uphill to a higher level, running
parallel to the water through fields above a
steep wooded bank (look out for a
shipwreck if the water is low). Crossing a
little burn, the path enters an extensive
patch of young trees before eventually
passing through a swing gate to enter
Balmerino at a group of houses on the
shore. Follow the road uphill through the
village to have a look at the 13th-century
ruin of Balmerino Abbey. There's not much
to see – particularly as the remaining
building is unsafe to enter – but tree
huggers will appreciate the massive
gnarled Spanish chestnut in the grounds,
estimated to be 450 years old.

Leaving the Abbey (and the Fife Coastal
Path) head west, cutting across a yard and
passing right of a big barn to pick up a
sketchy path leading into a wood.

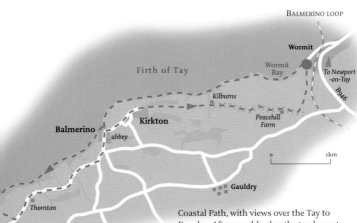

Firth of Tay

Wormit

Wormit
Bay

To Newport
-on-Tay

B946

Kilburns

Peacehill
Farm

Balmerino

Kirkton

abbey

Gauldry

0   1km

Thornton

Sometimes very muddy, the route runs parallel to the shore through extensive woodland – spectacular in autumn – crossing several little burns via a succession of wooden footbridges, a couple of which look set to fall down. After a long stretch just above the beach the path forks; stay with the Tay to follow the top of a steep bank, soon crossing another footbridge over a waterfall. The path now slants up left through pines to meet another trail; go right, still parallel with the coast, and over yet another footbridge. Marked with arrows, the route now curves left to follow a burn inland. At a sharp bend by a stone bridge go slightly left, as indicated by a wooden waymarker, leaving the trees to follow a beech hedge along a field margin to a junction with a well-used farm track.

Go left here, now back on the Fife

Coastal Path, with views over the Tay to Dundee. After roughly 2km the track meets a road at some cottages; follow this down to a T-junction just above Balmerino. There's a bus stop here for those wanting to cut things short. Walk down into the village again, turning right at Bridgend House. The road crosses a bridge and passes a cemetery to reach the neighbouring village of Kirkton. Take the first left, then at a crossroads by a red phonebox go left and immediately right onto a track. This soon shrinks to a path, climbing uphill into the young woods that you passed through earlier in the day. The path follows a parallel line to the coastal route, only higher up the hillside. It is muddy in places, but level. Once out of the woods skirt Kilburns Farm, taking a farm track straight on through fields to pass a pinewood and some houses. At Peacehill Farm follow signs for Wormit, straight on and then left, to join a waymarked path that runs downhill along field margins back to Wormit.

◀ Looking down the Tay from near Balmerino

Basking on Tentsmuir

Distance 7km **Time** 2 hours
Terrain a maze of flooded pools among
the dunes, then a long stretch on firm
sand and a level well-drained forest
track to finish **Map** OS Explorer 371
Access the nearest railway station and bus
stop is in Leuchars

**This is one of the finest beach walks in
the country, a mix of dense woodland
and open sands, enormous horizons
and spectacular wildlife**

Tentsmuir was once a marshy heath,
named after an encampment of sailors
shipwrecked in the 1780s (*Tents Moor*). From
the 1920s forestry has shrouded the
landscape under a blanket of Scots and
Corsican Pine, but the coastal fringes

remain natural and unspoilt, acres of
dunes, pools and sand banks that provide
a refuge for wildlife and rare plants. This
superb National Nature Reserve bustles
with migratory birds. At low tide grey and
common seals bask in herds, sometimes
hundreds strong. Please don't disturb
them by walking too close; dogs must be
kept on a tight lead.

Pass through the pay barrier on the road
from Leuchars to reach the Forestry
Commission's car park with toilets, picnic
area, (seasonal) food stalls and excellent
kids' playpark. Make your way east out of
the car park towards the dunes, then weave
through a maze of lagoons and marram
grass to reach the beach. Turn left,
following the coast past two WWII lookout

Firth of Tay

Tentsmuir
Point

Great
Slack

ice house

Tentsmuir Forest

Tentsmuir Sands

play
park

pay barrier

car park

To Leuchars

Fife Coastal Path &
Sustrans Route

0   1km

◀ Seals on the beach at Tentsmuir

posts and an old salmon fishing bothy. A path runs between the beach and the treeline, but the open beach beyond is better; there's an elemental simplicity to this huge sweep of sea, sky and clean brown sand.

After about 2km cross a little creek and then a line of concrete blocks, anti-tank defences now sinking into the beach. As the Tay Estuary grows closer the steep edge of the dunes begins to fall away on the left, opening onto a level area known as the Great Slack, where pools support a rich diversity of plants and wildflowers. Cut inland on a sketchy grassy path over this sandy heath, passing close to a windmill pump to go through another row of wartime anti-tank blocks. Their distance from the shore shows how far out to sea this part of the coastline has spread in the intervening decades as a result of deposition from the Tay.

Go through a wooden gate into the pines of Tentsmuir Forest, heading straight on to a T-junction. Turn left here onto a forestry track that runs south through the uniform banks of trees parallel with the coast. This is the official course of the Fife Coastal Path and a Sustrans bike route. Head straight on at the next junction to reach a picnic area beside a 19th-century grass-roofed ice house, built to keep locally caught salmon fresh before they were shipped south by covering them in layers of ice, collected from nearby lochs, and straw. The former fridge is now home to a colony of Natterer bats. From here you can follow the main path or weave through the trees on a more or less parallel path back to the car park.

Sands of St Andrews

Distance 7km **Time** 2 hours 30
Terrain pavements in town, then a long
stretch on soft sand along the beach and a
finish via the paved track of West Sands
Road **Map** OS Explorer 371 **Access** the
nearest train station is Leuchars, with
connecting buses; long-distance buses
connect St Andrews to Dundee, Kirkcaldy,
Dunfermline and Edinburgh (via
Glenrothes)

A linear there-and-back walk along East
Sands and West Sands, passing the
famous cathedral and castle ruins and
several other tourist attractions. The route
could be made shorter by omitting one of
the beaches, or longer by combining it
with the route overleaf.

Start at the East Sands car park (free) at
the end of Woodburn Place. There are
toilets, a playground and a snack bar here.
Given time it's nice to first stroll south
down the very attractive beach before
doubling back north along the sand to
reach the harbour breakwater. Climb the
grassy bank to a tarmac path, then cross a
bridge over a set of lock gates and follow
the harbour to the main pier, a stone wall
running far out to sea. It's possible to walk
out to the end of the pier, though young
children will need supervision. Back at the
harbour, follow a steep ramp onto the top
of the low cliffs, passing two cannons
pointing out to sea and following the old
stone wall protecting the cathedral
grounds (*see pages 64-65*). Stay on the

most significant golf-related collections in the world – well, what else would you expect from the home of the sport?

Follow the curving sea defence wall left around the car park to gain access to West Sands. This empty expanse famously starred in the opening sequence of the film *Chariots of Fire*, and it is deservedly popular for watersports and dog walks. Just inland are sand dunes and the celebrated links golf courses.

Stride out north along the shore for about 2.5km. As the beach begins to curve left into the mudflats at the mouth of the Eden Estuary, turn inland to a flagpole at the far end of a long track called West Sands Road. It is possible to continue from here on a footpath that runs into the estuary nature reserve, but this ends up being quite a long day out and most people will prefer to return south towards St Andrews. If the idea of retracing your steps doesn't appeal then walk back along West Sands Road, perhaps adding more variety by following some of the route through the town centre as described on the following pages.

walkway along the clifftop to reach the castle on its rocky promontory.

A ramp leads down to the beach below the castle, though there's nowhere to go from here. Continue west along The Scores, a road almost totally dominated by university buildings, passing the back of ancient St Salvator's College and the new Museum of the University of St Andrews. On nearing the far end of the road, bear right along clifftop railings to descend past the entrance to St Andrews Aquarium, home to sharks, seals, piranhas and more. Cross the big car park outside the British Golf Museum, which contains one of the

◀ On West Sands

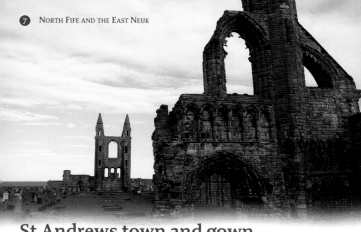

St Andrews town and gown

Distance 2.5km **Time** allow at least 2 hours – or a lot more if you're doing full justice to every museum and site of interest **Terrain** level pavements **Map** OS Explorer 371 **Access** the nearest train station is Leuchars, with connecting buses; buses also connect St Andrews to Dundee, Kirkcaldy, Dunfermline and Edinburgh (via Glenrothes); this route is based around St Andrews bus station

A sightseeing stroll around Fife's finest historic town, centre of Scotland's medieval church and home to the third oldest university in the English-speaking world, founded in 1413.

From the bus station, head right onto City Road, turning right at the first roundabout to visit the St Andrews Museum. Return to City Road and continue right to West Port, a handsome medieval gateway. This leads onto South Street, home to many grand old houses. Pass historic Louden's Close and the remains of Blackfriars Chapel outside Madras College to reach Holy Trinity Church, where Protestant firebrand John Knox first preached. Dating from 1410, the square tower once housed 'errant' women, and the curfew bell is still sounded at 8pm every night. A little further down South Street, on the right, is St Mary's College; the iron gates open onto a beautiful quadrangle of historic buildings and gardens – there's no public access to the university departments, but the grounds are fair game. Continue down South Street; the Byre Theatre can be accessed through an alley on the right, passing a house where the illustrious Victorian alpinist James David Forbes once lived, the scientist credited with discovering that glaciers are moving rivers of ice. Passing a ruined gateway to Pends Road,

◄ St Andrews Cathedral

South Street now leads to the cathedral.

For centuries the centre of Scottish religious life, this once-grand building was sacked during the Reformation – Scotland's Taliban-esque era of extremist intolerance and cultural vandalism – and then plundered for stone by local housebuilders. Only a gaunt shell now remains. It's fascinating to poke about the ruins and graves. The adjacent 11th-century monolith of St Rule's Tower survives, and the views from the top are unrivalled (entrance fee). From the cathedral follow North Street, dropping into the St Andrews Preservation Trust Museum, housed in a gorgeous 17th-century building (entry free – donations welcome). Now go right down

North Castle Street to the castle, which served as the main residence of St Andrews' bishops and even a couple of kings (entry fee). The extensive ruins stand on a low cliffy headland, and include an unusual bottle dungeon and evidence of siege warfare. Follow The Scores past university buildings to MUSA, the new Museum of the University of St Andrews, which houses a huge collection of treasures (entry free, and well worth it).

Back on The Scores, cut left down Butts Wynd, a narrow alley signed for the town centre. From here it's possible to enter the magnificent quadrangle of St Salvator's College with its pillared cloister and medieval chapel tower. Exit through a stone arch onto North Street. Head right, past the cinema, then turn left along Abbotsford Crescent, an elegant Georgian residential street that leads back to City Road.

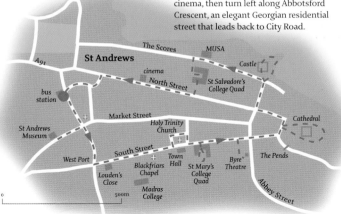

Hill of Tarvit

Distance 4km **Time** if visiting the house
and Scotstarvit Tower as well as the
woodland walks, allow at least 3 hours;
the house interior is closed in winter, but
the grounds remain open year round
Terrain pushchair-friendly garden paths
and well-signed trails – except for the
ascent of Wemyss Hill, which is a very
steep grass slope **Map** OS Explorer 370
Access bus or train to Cupar, then bus to
Craigrothie, about 1km walk from Hill of
Tarvit's drive

Stroll the well-kept gardens, serene
parklands and palatial interior of a grand
Edwardian country pile, with an optional
leg to nearby Scotstarvit Tower, a 16th-
century fortified towerhouse.

The trails on Hill of Tarvit Estate are laid
out in three separate loops, Woodland
Walk, Centenary Walk and Hilltop Walk.
Each could be done alone, but this route
combines them all for a fuller flavour.
An information leaflet and route map is
available at the pay and display car park at
the end of the main drive. For an insight
into the luxurious habits of Edwardian
gentry first check out the house itself, with
its fine collection of period interiors and
furniture. Now wander the elegant terraced
lawns, before making your way down
steps in front of the house and bearing
left to reach a track junction outside the
old stable block.

Go straight on, following the sign for
Woodland Walk. The trail runs through a

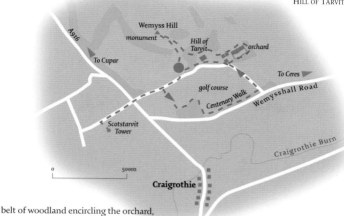

belt of woodland encircling the orchard, soon looping back towards the house. In late winter there are banks of snowdrops. Having passed just right of some estate workers' cottages look out for a turn-off on the right, which is followed up into the trees. The path soon joins a wider trail, continuing leftwards behind the garden wall. At a junction outside the huge wrought iron garden gate, turn right onto the Hilltop Walk (optional). Ascend to the edge of the woods, cross a stile and climb the steep grassy slope (path indistinct), bearing left beside a stand of trees for the final climb to the monument crowning the summit of Wemyss Hill (Hill of Tarvit according to OS Explorer maps). Plaques give names to the many landmarks that can be seen, from the Lammermuirs to the Cairngorms.

In descent, bear slightly right of the ascent line to climb a different stile, leading to an alternative woodland path that runs downhill directly to the car park.

Now for another optional leg, to Scotstarvit Tower. First borrow the keys from the reception desk in the main house, then head along the driveway, leaving the estate, crossing the A916 and continuing on the long straight farm track to reach the tower, an imposing block of masonry with excellent views from its lofty parapet.

If you're not yet tired, then the Centenary Walk makes a leafy finale. Return the way you came towards the car park, and about halfway along the drive turn right onto the waymarked trail that runs alongside the 'hickory' golf course. Shortly, a turn-off left leads through a little gate, up to a low wooded rise and around the base of a turreted doocot. Continue through trees, turning left at a junction, crossing another corner of the golf course and re-entering woods beside a minor road to reach the gates of another drive. This leads back to the house.

Ceres and Craighall Den

Distance 3km **Time** 1 hour 30
Terrain the path from Ceres to the top end
of Craighall Den can be muddy in winter
and overgrown in summer; the walk
through the Den itself is gentler
underfoot; those wanting an easier route
could just visit the Den as a linear walk
from the car park at its bottom end
Map OS Explorer 370 **Access** buses from
Cupar to Leven and St Andrews to
Auchtermuchty stop at Ceres

A short rural walk taking in a quaint
village, once a centre of the linen industry,
and a strip of ancient woods along the
gorge of a fast-flowing burn.

Start at the car park on the village green
in the charming historic centre of Ceres,
opposite the Fife Folk Museum. Housed in
the old tollbooth and adjacent weavers'
cottages, the museum celebrates the
industry, culture and agriculture of the
region, and deserves a look before setting
out on the walk (except in winter, when
the curators are hibernating). The village
hosts the oldest free Highland Games in
Scotland, said to have been held every year
since the Battle of Bannockburn in 1314.

Cross the venerable Bishop's Bridge over
the burn, turn left beside the museum and
then right past the old dairy (now a house)
and another village green, this one with a
children's playground. Go right onto
Anstruther Road, and at the next bend
split right onto a farm track signed for
Craighall Den. This immediately bends
right; go straight on here, on a muddy path
between hedgerows. Following field
margins and passing through three
wooden swing gates, the path climbs

◀ Bishop's Bridge in Ceres

gently to pass a house on a hill. Skirt just right of the farm buildings at Craighall to reach a signpost on the lip of the cleft of Craighall Den, a ribbon of ancient woodland granted SSSI status for its wildflowers and wildlife.

Before venturing into the woods it's worth first heading past the farmhouse, where a side path cuts down rightwards to loop around an interesting old limekiln. Return to the signpost and carry on along the top of the Den, soon reaching a turn-off which drops leftwards to meet Craighall Burn by a little cascade and pool. Go back up the way you came, or continue briefly downstream, where a fainter path climbs steeply across the slope to rejoin the main trail. This soon descends to the bottom of the Den, where there's a choice of two parallel paths; it's nicer to stay close to the burn, though the trails soon merge again. Cross a wooden bridge to reach the car park at the lower end of the Den.

Turning right, steps lead up to a track; go left here, then right through a swing gate onto a narrow path signed for Ceres. This runs along a wooded bank between fields before passing a barn and a row of back gardens to reach Anstruther Road near the point that you left it. For the sake of variation, walk around the right side of the green with the playground, turning left onto St Andrews Road to pass the excellent Ceres Inn. Look out on the left for The Provost, a jolly little 18th-century statue depicting the Reverend Thomas Buchanan, who served as the last church provost of Ceres in 1578.

Exploring Dura Den

Distance 3.5km **Time** 2 hours 30
Terrain a strenuous trip for more able
walkers; older kids will love it; the really
tough stretch along the western side of
Dura Den could be avoided by sticking to
the road opposite **Map** OS Explorer 370
Access bus from Cupar to Kemback or
St Andrews to Pitscottie

**This surprisingly challenging route
traces obscure byways through woods
and fields to finish along the wild side of
the scenic gorge of Dura Den – machete
useful, sense of adventure essential.**

Dura Den was significant in the early
development of palaeontology, its soft
sandstone yielding spectacular fossils in
the 19th century. With its thick woods and
impressive waterfalls, the Den is a popular
beauty spot, yet footpaths are few.
Thoroughly exploring it means going
seriously off-road.

From Kemback church hall car park, walk
down the road past a two-tiered waterfall,
turning right onto a road signed for
Kemback. Follow this uphill very briefly,
then take a faint path right into the trees
above Dura Den, passing the Auld Kirk of
Kemback on the other side of the cemetery
wall. The path soon cuts away from the
main gorge, following a small burn to
meet a track by two cottages. Here a path
leads right into a little wooded fold. Pass
(but don't cross) the remains of a
packhorse bridge, turning slightly left
steeply uphill to join a better-defined trail.
This cuts right across the thickly wooded
hillside to approach Blebo House.

Instead of entering the private garden,
cut left along the fence to reach a broader,

muddier track. Go right along this, soon forking right to pass some cottages by the driveway to Blebo House. Head towards the B939 and, where the drive kinks, turn right onto a path by a holly hedge. Though the 1:25,000 OS map clearly marks this path, it's rather less obvious on the ground. Go straight on downhill through a pasture. Step through an old iron gate into another field, following its rough right-hand margin over a low rise. A gate in the far corner has become heavily overgrown, so step through the fence on the right to pick up a worn trail down through banks of gorse into an old gravel quarry. Ford a burn and head straight on to reach old farm buildings on the lip of Dura Den. A clearer track now descends right to meet the road opposite a grand house.

The easier option is to follow the pavement back to the car park. Alternatively, just to the left is a wooden footbridge over a raging weir. A sign warns that this is dangerous; while no guidebook could responsibly recommend crossing it many people clearly do without coming to grief. It is entirely up to you. Those who choose to cross might then like to follow a path rightwards through woods on the west side of the Den, with views of a substantial waterfall. On meeting a side burn the best-used path cuts left but a fainter, more adventurous trail goes right. Once above the main gorge, descend steeply left to cross the small burn, continuing across a corner of field to re-enter the woods, a veritable Lost World. Looking out for birds, deer and dinosaurs, follow a raised bank parallel with Ceres Burn, clambering through undergrowth and fallen trees. The bank leads to a disused chimney stack beside a private back garden. Now climb steeply left to reach the western rim of Dura Den. Walk along the field margin to meet a minor road, which leads right to Kemback Bridge not far from the car park.

Keil's Den and Largo Law

Distance 8km Time 3 hours
Terrain pavements, paths and farm
tracks, with one very steep ascent and
descent Map OS Explorer 370
Access regular buses between St
Andrews and Edinburgh and between St
Andrews and Leven stop in Lower Largo
and Upper Largo

Two olde worlde villages, a ribbon of
ancient woodland and the most
prominent hill in the East Neuk, with an
inspiring outlook over the Forth.

Start at the car park at the east end of
Lower Largo's Main Street and walk west
back along the winding road to an old
railway bridge over a burn. Turn right
uphill to reach a crossroads at the village
edge. Go straight on along a minor road
until nearly level with a caravan park; turn
left at the first opportunity on a footpath
signed for Keil's Den. Owned and managed
by the Woodland Trust, this ribbon of

ancient woodland cloaking a steep-sided
little glen is preserved for walkers and
wildlife. It is a peaceful spot, and
particularly worth visiting in spring for the
bluebells. Entering the glen, turn right
onto a smaller path that hugs the edge of
the woods east of the burn, soon arriving
at a fork. The quick route goes straight on,
but it's nicer to prolong the woodland
walking by descending leftwards, crossing
the burn on a footbridge and climbing to
reach the level of the surrounding
farmland. Turn right onto the path along
the western flank of the glen for nearly
1km, eventually reaching a minor road.
To avoid having to ford the burn, turn right
onto the tarmac, climbing a hill to reach a
lay-by. Largo Law looks inviting from here,
but unfortunately the local landowner is
hostile to public access on this flank.
Instead pick up a path on the right, re-
entering Keil's Den and briefly following its
east edge again, this time heading in the

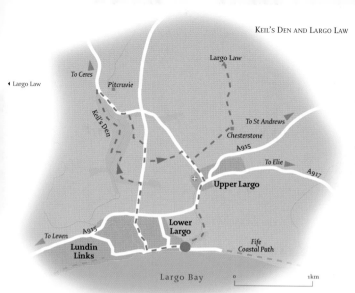

◄ Largo Law

Largo Law

To Ceres

Pitcruvie

Keil's Den

To St Andrews

Chesterstone

A915

To Elie

A917

✚ **Upper Largo**

Lower Largo

To Leven A915

Lundin Links

Fife Coastal Path

Largo Bay

0   1km

direction of Lower Largo. A farm track can soon be seen on the left; follow this, cutting across fields to reach the minor road by the caravan park. Go straight over the road onto another track that brings you out at the cemetery on the outskirts of Upper Largo. This is the start point for the only official route up the Law.

The hill-bound track cuts between the cemetery and the primary school, a middle way between the symbolic bookends of life's story. A sign warns that dogs are not permitted. Further signs point the way, straight on past a cottage and then left through a farmyard. Beyond this, the slope soon steepens, the track becoming a path that makes an uncompromisingly brutal full frontal attack on the hill's gorse-

swathed defences. It can be slippery when wet, but the breezy foresummit is soon won. The main top is just beyond a little saddle, crowned with a trig point and a cairn. Largo Law is a volcanic plug standing in isolation, which makes it a brilliant viewpoint overlooking the rolling East Neuk and the Forth.

Return the same way to Upper Largo, where you might fancy a detour to check out either the old church or the welcoming pub, depending which sort of spirit interests you more. From the centre of the village, head south along the main road. At a sharp bend take a footpath on the left, following Largo Burn through trees to reach the east end of Lower Largo not far from the car park.

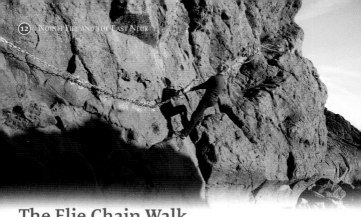

The Elie Chain Walk

Distance 3km **Time** 2 hours
Terrain strenuous rock clambering along
a rugged stretch of coastline: the
difficulty approximately equates to a
Grade 2 mountain scramble, and
although the climbing is assisted with
chains there are places from which it
would be very unpleasant to fall; above
the Chain Walk is an unclimbable cliff, so
there's no sensible escape other than to
continue the route to the end. Rising
tides could cut you off: before setting out
consult the tide table for Anstruther or
Methil at www.ukho.gov.uk/easytide; you
have a window of about two hours either
side of low water **Map** OS Explorer 371
Access access by bus is possible if you
start from Earlsferry instead of Shell Bay

An Alpine style *via ferrata* in a unique
coastal setting, the Elie Chain Walk is
the most strenuous and exciting route
in Fife – an adventurous outing for
budding mountaineers.

From the public car park just inland
from Shell Bay, head west, passing a
caravan park and bearing left to reach the
shore. Turn left onto the Fife Coastal Path,
crossing a footbridge and winding along
the grassy bluffs above the rocks and sand
of Shell Bay. Branch right at a fork to reach
the headland. The craggy coastline ahead
can look particularly daunting if southerly
winds are piling waves into the rocks. Stay
with the coastal path to ascend over the
first section of big cliffs, looking out for
an unsigned path that splits off right to
descend steep grass onto a level area,
where a sign marks the start of the Elie
Chain Walk. Do not proceed without
reliable tide information.

Clamber east over the rocks to reach the
first chain, leading down into a pebble-
floored inlet at the mouth of a sea cave.
If the sea already threatens to cover this
inlet, turn back. Ahead is a horizontal
chained section, and then a steep ascent
of a chain and carved footholds leading

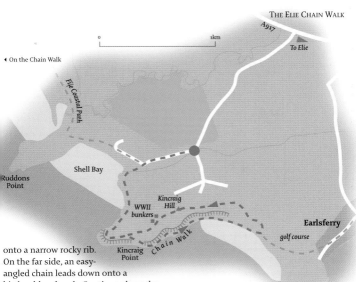

◀ On the Chain Walk

onto a narrow rocky rib.
On the far side, an easy-
angled chain leads down onto a
big bouldery beach. Continue along the
foot of the cliffs, passing weird rock
pinnacles out on a wave-washed platform.
Next comes a steep groove, the first
couple of metres feeling almost
overhanging: luckily there's a chain and
carved footholds. Descend a short step
onto another boulder beach below a
distinctive columnar crag.

Cross wave-sculpted rocks onto the next
prominent headland, ascending just left
of a natural cliff arch to reach the edge of
a very pronounced inlet. Descend
diagonally to the rubble-covered floor –
you'll be thankful for the chain and carved
steps. Now traverse horizontally right
along the vertical far wall using another
welcome chain and carved footholds –
particularly exciting if the waves are

threatening to lick your feet (don't
intentionally time things this tight).
A short 'ladder' of carved holds without
the benefit of a chain leads down to flatter
rocks at the end of the Chain Walk.

Stride along the golden sand towards
Earlsferry. Soon ascend wooden steps on
the left to follow signs for the Fife Coastal
Path, climbing onto the clifftop of
Kincraig Hill. Walk west along the edge
past crumbling wartime bunkers, with
stirring views down to the Chain Walk.
From a prominent radio antenna, it's
possible to descend right on a track
leading directly back to the car park.
But frankly it's nicer to keep descending
gradually west to retrace your steps
around Shell Bay.

Conquering Kellie Castle and Law

Distance 6km **Time** 2 hours 30 to get the best out of the castle and walled garden **Terrain** easy paths, quiet country roads, farm tracks and open hillside **Map** OS Explorer 371 **Access** 'Flexibus' pickup available from local villages

Combine a visit to the wooded grounds and walled garden of this showpiece of traditional Scottish architecture with a longer walk up Kellie Law for views over the Firth of Forth.

An imposing turreted baronial-style fortified house with parts dating from the 1300s, Kellie Castle has a fascinating history. It is said to be haunted, and on a dreich day it certainly looks the part. The castle was home to one of Robert the Bruce's daughters, and later became the seat of the Earls of Kellie, the fifth of whom fought on the wrong side at

Culloden and spent a summer hiding out in a beech tree in the grounds for his pains. In the 19th century the Lorimer family bought the castle, which became a big influence on the style of famous Arts and Crafts architect Robert Lorimer. The stables now house an exhibition of the work of his sculptor son Hew. The castle interior boasts fine furniture, one of the oldest ornamental plaster ceilings in Scotland and rare 17th-century painted panelling. Outside is a superb walled garden, where fruit and vegetables are sold in season. The National Trust for Scotland now runs the castle. The grounds and garden are open year round; the castle from April to October. There is also a cosy tearoom and gift shop.

From the pay and display car park, go through the gate, past an info display board and left over a footbridge across a

◀ Kellie Castle

burn. A woodland path leads to a pond and small adventure playground, where the path curves right to cross the burn. To visit the gardens (payment by honesty box), go round the front of the castle and the former stables. This sheltered haven is beautifully laid out with dwarf box hedges, ornamental borders, rose arches, fruit trees and even a miniature secret garden, all overlooked by the stern turrets of the castle. Return to the terrace at the front, with its view over the Firth of Forth and head left around the garden wall to a picnic meadow. If you just want to make a short loop of the castle, a path continues behind the walled garden, passing a hide and bird feeders before emerging by the toilet roundhouse.

For a longer day out, you can climb the low ridge of Kellie Law behind the castle.

Exit the picnic meadow by the cottage at the far end and follow the access track to a quiet road. Turn right and follow this to the junction for the picturesque hamlet of Carnbee. Carry on up the hill and turn left on a dirt farm road just after the red pantiled farm buildings: this gives open views across arable land to the Isle of May and Bass Rock. When a farm gate is reached and the dirt road swings right, continue straight ahead over open ground to reach the summit triangulation pillar.

Come down by the recently-built farm road which skirts Gillingshill and turn left on the road to Arncroach. A pleasant detour can be made here into Gillingshill Nature Reserve: the reservoir sits at the top of the reserve with a lovely view out across the Forth. Enter on the right just past the drive to Gillingshill and follow the path down through a wooded gorge, rejoining the road at a parking area. Carry on to Arncroach, where the first left takes you back along the road behind the castle.

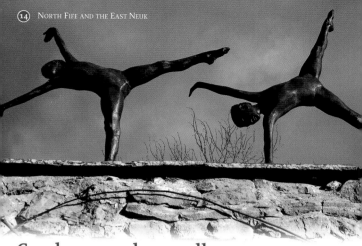

Cambo snowdrop walk

Distance 2km **Time** for full effect allow
at least 2 hours **Terrain** well-made
woodland trails, sometimes a little
muddy, and level garden paths;
pushchair friendly, except for the short
flight of steps close to the sea (which is
entirely avoidable) **Map** OS Explorer 371
Access buses from Crail to St Andrews
pass the front gates of the drive; there's
a bus stop in both directions

A grand stately home, with a network
of paths through a wooded den and one
of the finest gardens in the country.
Cambo's nationally famous snowdrop
collection is best seen in late winter
but the garden is spectacular at any
time of year.

From the gates on the A917, follow the
drive through the woods to reach the cark

park opposite the visitor centre, shop,
heritage exhibition, plant sales area and
café housed in the old stables of the
Cambo estate.

The small charge for entry to the
gardens also goes towards upkeep of the
wonderful walled garden, an oasis of
peace, beautifully laid around Cambo
Burn. Wander at will through the grid of
paths between banks of pastel-shaded
grasses, ornamental vegetable plots, trees
and a bewildering variety of flowers. In
summer the air is alive with butterflies
and dragonflies.

Leaving the garden by the north wall
follow the signs to the sea and stay left of
the burn as it heads down to Cambo Ness.
Sculptures are dotted around in the trees;
in February and early March the ground is

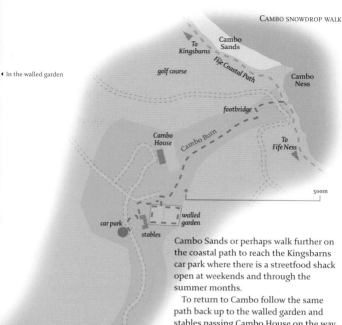

◀ In the walled garden

Cambo Sands or perhaps walk further on the coastal path to reach the Kingsbarns car park where there is a streetfood shack open at weekends and through the summer months.

To return to Cambo follow the same path back up to the walled garden and stables passing Cambo House on the way. The impressive Victorian pile was built to replace the fire-gutted medieval original. The estate has been in the Erskine family for over 300 years and is a great example of a model picturesque estate. The buildings of the estate also include a carriage house, coach house, mausoleum, dovecote, various lodges and two farms.

Carry on past the stable block and down the main drive to have a look at the estate's Tamworth pigs (there may be windfall apples available at the stable yard to feed them with) or spend some time exploring the other woodland walks before returning to the car park.

carpeted with a wonderful collection of snowdrop varieties. Passing several little waterfalls, the trail crosses over to the other side of the burn before joining up with the Fife Coastal Path.

To extend the walk, turn left to enjoy

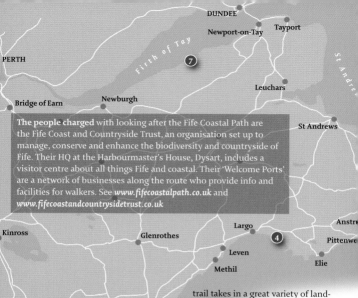

The people charged with looking after the Fife Coastal Path are the Fife Coast and Countryside Trust, an organisation set up to manage, conserve and enhance the biodiversity and countryside of Fife. Their HQ at the Harbourmaster's House, Dysart, includes a visitor centre about all things Fife and coastal. Their 'Welcome Ports' are a network of businesses along the route who provide info and facilities for walkers. See www.fifecoastalpath.co.uk and www.fifecoastandcountrysidetrust.co.uk

Treading the entirety of the Kingdom's seaward fringes from Kincardine on the Forth to Newburgh on the Tay, the Fife Coastal Path is one of the classic long-distance walks of Scotland. Over its winding length – more than 180km – the trail takes in a great variety of land- and seascapes, blending urban and rural, past and present, in a fascinating picture of east coast life. The beauty of Fife's coast is its diversity. Along the sheltered Inner Forth, woods and fields contrast with bustling towns – each with its own distinct character – and the trappings of centuries of heavy industry. Views are dominated by the iconic Forth Bridges, the Pentland Hills and Edinburgh's skyline.

Out in the East Neuk the horizons are broader and breezier. The open sea sucks at a shoreline of low reefs and sandy bays, along which are strung some of the best preserved historic harbour villages in the country. Beyond the grand town of St Andrews the coast's character changes

On the seafront at Pittenweem ▶

Fife Coastal Path Highlights

Crail

once more. Here are the mudflats of the Eden estuary and the sweeping sands of Tentsmuir, havens for wildlife. The silvery Firth of Tay rounds things off in style, with more famous bridges and a city skyline of its own – Dundee backed by the rolling Sidlaws.

To walk the entire Coastal Path in one go would be a week well spent. Featured here are seven edited highlights which can be tackled as linear day walks, assisted for the most part by excellent transport links.

Inverkeithing to Aberdour

**Distance 8km Time 2 hours 30
Terrain** a mix of good footpath, tarmac
tracks and some road walking; the route
is well signposted throughout
Map OS Explorer 367 **Access** the start of
this section of the coastal path is easily
accessed from Inverkeithing station, and
it finishes at Aberdour station

**An easy walk along a wiggly coastline,
with a variety of town and country,
industry and history.**

As the crow flaps or the train chugs, it's
not far from the ancient burgh of
Inverkeithing to historic Aberdour; but
winding along a succession of bays and
headlands, the seaside route is both longer
and more worthwhile. From Inverkeithing
station, head south onto the bridge over
the railway, where a flight of steps leads
down to a paved walk past a block of flats
and alongside Pinkerton Burn to reach

the curving residential street of Preston
Crescent, close to the bayside sports
ground. You're now officially on the Fife
Coastal Path. Beyond a goods yard, a path
leads over a wide gravelly area in the
mouth of a disused quarry. Passing a
derelict pier, continue along the coast
with good views of the Forth Rail Bridge.
With the sea on one side and a wooded
slope on the other, the easy level path
soon leads to the modern housing
development of St David's Harbour, one
of the posher bits of Dalgety Bay. The town
is an unusual mix of residential suburbia
and beautiful shoreline.

Follow the coast road up a slight rise
past a row of generously-proportioned
houses, before turning right onto a signed
footpath. Several little ups, downs and
wiggles now follow as the route traces the
indented headland that most of the

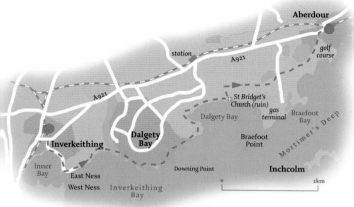

town sits on. It must be nice to have a beach at the end of your garden. A number of flights of steps make this section wheelchair and pushchair unfriendly, though you could always try negotiating the warren of identical-looking residential streets just inland.

On reaching a small wooded patch at the neck of a rocky cape, the official route turns briefly inland, though it's better to stay close to the beach around the rim of Donibristle Bay, passing an old house to reach a second smaller bay. Dalgety Bay Sailing Club sits at the mouth of a third much larger bay just beyond (this is Dalgety Bay itself), and is noted for turning out accomplished sailors. Again the official route veers briefly away from the beach, and again it's nicer not to. Follow the pretty wooded shore around the bay; at low spring tides a wide expanse of mudflats is exposed, alive with the cries of wading birds. After approximately 1km

of easy walking between the beach and the back gardens, the coastal path reaches St Bridget's Church, an atmospheric medieval ruin that's well worth exploring.

The route now turns inland, following a surfaced track slightly uphill before branching right on a long straight tarmac section through the fields, with a breezy outlook over the Forth to the Pentland Hills. Pass Braefoot Bay Gas Terminal, dipping under the plant access road to enter the woods backing onto Aberdour Golf Club. The seaward views from here are beautiful, and Aberdour is reached too soon. Turn right onto the High Street, passing the village bakers to reach the train station. Just right of the station driveway are the gates to Aberdour Castle. Dating from as early as the 12th century, this well-kept Historic Scotland site makes a fascinating diversion; next door is the equally ancient and wonderful Norman church of St Fillan's.

◀ Aberdour harbour

Aberdour to Kinghorn

Distance 9.5km **Time** 3 hours
Terrain gentle going on gravel paths and
pavements, with one steep ascent over
Hawkcraig Point that could be avoided by
the less able **Map** OS Explorer 367
Access though there are plenty of buses,
the route is probably best accessed by
train; there's a station at the start and
finish, and another at the midway point

**Sandy beaches, stands of beeches,
fascinating old coastal towns and superb
Forth views.**

From Aberdour's immaculately kept
station, head west past the bakery, then
turn left down Shore Road. Pass the Cedar
Inn, walking downhill to meet the sea at
beautiful Black Sands – a good place for a
swim. Turning left, the coastal path curves
around Aberdour's small stone-walled
harbour. The path stays with the coastline,
cutting across a steep wooded slope
towards a cluster of buildings including
the Forth View Hotel (superb seafood). The
OS Explorer map shows the coastal path
sticking with the shore around Hawkcraig
Point, but in reality it doesn't. Just before
reaching the hotel, the coastal path cuts up
leftwards, climbing a winding stone
stairway to emerge on the breezy clifftop, a
popular rock climbing venue. Descend
gently east (can be muddy), then turn left

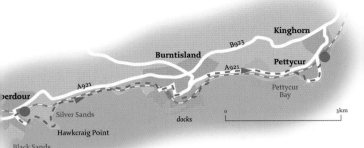

on a roadway leading to the famous Silver Sands, one of the best little beaches in Fife.

At the far end of the bay, turn right onto a gravel path sandwiched between the railway and the sea, a very pretty wooded stretch. Across the water is the Edinburgh skyline, and ahead the boatyards of Burntisland; seals can often be seen basking on the rocks. Soon the path ducks under the railway to continue through woods on its landward side. There's a little bridge over a waterfall, beyond which the path continues to Burntisland, hemmed in between fences and walls. Enter the ancient royal burgh of Burntisland at a recently built housing estate. Pass back under the railway, skirting an artificial lagoon and following signs left, right and left again to pass 16th-century Rossend Castle. Go through an old stone gateway, pass over the railway and turn right down East Broomhill Road, then left onto the High Street. It is worth diverting right up Kirkgate to see the unusual pre-

Reformation Parish Church, continuing east along East Leven Street and Lammerlaws Road to reach the Beacon Leisure Centre on the sandy sweep of Burntisland Beach.

At low water it's best to walk to Kinghorn across the immaculate sands, but watch out for rising tides! The official path sticks to solid ground, first on the concrete promenade and then further inland, following a pavement along the A921 beneath wooded hillsides, passing a monument to King Alexander III, killed here in a riding accident in 1286. The road ascends to pass Pettycur Bay Caravan Park. At the entrance to Sandhills Caravan Park on the right, it is best to leave the official coastal path route, descending a narrow footpath to the beach, with its sand dunes, cliffs and an old stone harbour. Beyond the bay, follow a residential street just inland until it's possible to descend a little path on the right which crosses the steep brae above the sea to reach Kinghorn's main beach beside the lifeboat station. The railway station is just uphill behind the historic waterfront houses.

◀ On the way to Kinghorn from Aberdour

85

Kirkcaldy to East Wemyss

Distance 7.5km **Time** 3 hours
Terrain a well-surfaced, clearly signed
path throughout; Ravenscraig Park and
Dysart are pushchair friendly, but the
steep steps on the way to West Wemyss
aren't Map OS Explorer 367 **Access bus or**
train to Kirkcaldy; regular buses run
between here and East Wemyss, making
this a very convenient linear walk

An easy walk along Kirkcaldy's coal
coast, with a mix of parkland, woods,
industrial heritage and ancient history.

Start at the car park just off Nether
Street, close to the impressive remains of
Ravenscraig Castle. Built in the 1460s for
James II, the castle was designed to
withstand the strongest artillery of its day.

Public access is limited. The official route
of the coastal path runs along the main
road to enter Ravenscraig Park; it's nicer to
follow a path from the seaward side of
the car park, walking through trees to a
T-junction beneath the ramparts. Go right
down cobbled steps to the base of the
craggy cape on which the castle sits, and
take a path around the foot of the rocks to
a secluded bay overlooked by the
fortifications. Pass a deep cave and a yellow
cliff, then climb stone steps beside a
doocot to enter Ravenscraig Park, a green
oasis that feels all the more special for its
proximity to downtown Kirkcaldy.

Clearly signed, the coastal path runs
through woods above the rocky shore,
which is crowned with a wiggling stone
wall. After about 1km, the path reaches the
mouth of a tunnel leading into Dysart's
sheltered harbour. Once a bustling port
exporting salt and coal, this ancient royal
burgh has many fascinating buildings

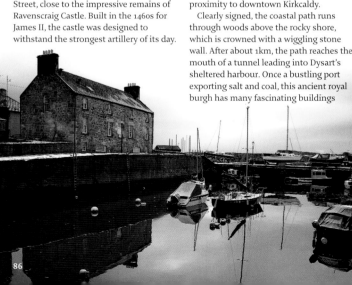

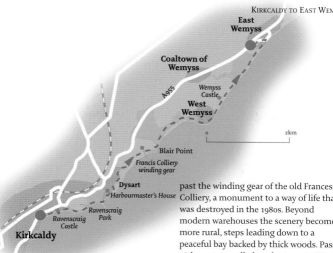

including the part-defensive, part-ecclesiastical 24m tower of St Serf's Church, and the 16th-century Tolbooth. Marked with brass plaques in the pavement, the Dysart Town Trail visits the main sites – a worthwhile hour-long detour. The coastal path now passes the 18th-century Harbourmaster's House, HQ for the Fife Coast and Countryside Trust, a charity set up to oversee the path you're walking today. Downstairs, a well-thought-out visitor centre offers insights into the history and natural history of Fife's coast; on the ground floor is an excellent coffee shop.

The route continues along a row of stone houses, turning left up steps, then right past blocks of flats and through a park above the sea. Leaving Dysart, continue past the winding gear of the old Frances Colliery, a monument to a way of life that was destroyed in the 1980s. Beyond modern warehouses the scenery becomes more rural, steps leading down to a peaceful bay backed by thick woods. Pass a 16th-century walled garden to enter West Wemyss by a grand building, formerly a miners' institute. Follow the sea defences out of the village, where a long straight section leads beneath crag-top Wemyss Castle, a gargantuan private residence. Passing scattered woods, the path kinks inland briefly behind a scrapyard to enter East Wemyss. The name Wemyss derives from the Gaelic *uaimh*, 'caves'; a group of little caverns is scattered along the coast just beyond the village. These contain an archaeological treasure house of carvings spanning the ages from 2-3000BC to the Pictish 8th century, and are well worth a look – though some are deemed unsafe to enter. Walk back west on Main Street, following the curving road uphill past a wooded burn to reach the A955. Buses to Kirkcaldy stop outside a little hut just opposite the bank.

◀ Dysart Harbour in winter

Lower Largo to St Monans

**Distance 13km Time 4 hours 30
Terrain an easy and well-signed path all
the way, with the option to cut things
short at Elie Map OS Explorer 371
Access from Lower Largo to Crail, all the
East Neuk coastal villages are linked
by buses that run between St Andrews
and Edinburgh or between Leven and
St Andrews**

**Sand dunes, rocky coves and stone-
built villages make this the perfect
introduction to the East Neuk.**

Birthplace of Alexander Selkirk, model
for Defoe's *Robinson Crusoe*, the historic
village of Lower Largo has a fascinating
maritime past. It's worth wandering down
the main street that winds between stone
houses, built squat against the keen North
Sea breeze. Then, from the car park near
the east end of the village, follow the
broad shingly beach eastwards, reaching

an area of sand dunes guarded by WWII
gun emplacements after nearly 2km. The
spacious sandy sweep of Largo Bay leads
on towards the low headland of Kincraig
Point. The official path stays above the
high water line, though it's nicer to tread
the firm golden sand.

A little before Ruddons Point, the trail
doglegs inland, as indicated by a signpost,
a detour worth making to avoid having to
wade a creek. After crossing two
footbridges, the path enters Shell Bay
Caravan Park to reach the east side of the
cove of the same name. Before the caravan
invasion, this sheltered little lagoon would
have been very unspoilt, disturbed only by
the cries of wading birds and the rumble of
distant breakers. Continue around the bay
to reach Kincraig Point, a rugged headland
sucked by the sea. The Chain Walk (*see page
74*) follows an exciting course around the
base of the cliffs, but if strenuous rock

◀ On the beach at Earlsferry

scrambling isn't your thing then stay with the conventional path, which climbs fairly steeply up Kincraig Hill, following the top of the cliffs with superb views over the wide Forth to distant Lothian.

Beyond transmitter masts and wartime bunkers, the path descends back to shore level, following a beautiful sandy bay backed by a golf course to reach the little headland at the southern end of Earlsferry. Despite a thriving economy based around fishing and maritime trade, this former royal burgh was gradually eclipsed by its near neighbour Elie, and the two were formally merged in 1930. Golf and tourism are the mainstays these days. Follow Earlsferry's historic high street to reach the middle of Elie itself, where options for lunch include a deli and a couple of excellent pubs. Spend some time exploring

the quiet streets of this typical East Neuk village before continuing towards St Monans. From the village green, the coastal path turns right to reach Elie harbour. Follow signs east along the coast, crossing the neck of Elie Ness to reach the dunes of the East Links, backing a stretch of rocky coastline overlooked by the Lady's Tower, an 18th-century summerhouse.

The path continues northeast along this unspoilt shoreline – not far from the main coast road, and yet surprisingly secluded. Pass through the remains of Ardross Castle (very ruined indeed), and some crumbly little crags, to reach Newark Castle standing sentinel on a steep bluff. The pretty fishing village of St Monans is just beyond, reached either by a shoreline low tide route or an inland high tide option. This is yet another East Neuk village that merits a bit of time, particularly down by the harbour. If returning home on the bus, walk uphill to the main road.

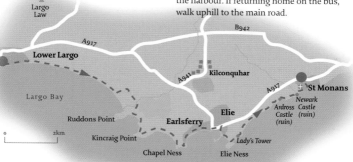

St Monans to Crail

Distance 12km **Time** 4 hours **Terrain** an easy well-signed path all the way, with options to shorten the route at Pittenweem and Anstruther; buggy-pushers might struggle in places **Map** OS Explorer 371 **Access** from Lower Largo to Crail, all the East Neuk coastal villages are linked by buses that run between St Andrews and Edinburgh or between Leven and St Andrews

Grassy coastal walking links these four famous villages, venerable royal burghs with picturesque waterfronts and solid East Neuk architecture.

From the A917, walk downhill through St Monans to the harbour, once a thriving fishing and boatbuilding centre but now sadly quiet. First head west along The Shore, the seafront lined with old stone houses, past the excellent seafood restaurant to the parish church, a 14th-century marvel. Heading back east, go

uphill behind the old grey boatshed, turning right down Rose Street. The coastal path soon leaves the village to reach a restored windmill (keys for which can be borrowed at the post office or Spar shop). In the 18th century this pumped water for salt pans, now just grassy hummocks below the windmill. The onward path to Pittenweem follows a bank above a shoreline of rocky ribs, and can be muddy after rain.

Passing the concrete steps of an old bathing pool, the route climbs to a playground on a headland. It then immediately descends again from behind a shelter, curving around a small bay to reach Pittenweem's charming seafront. Unusually for the East Neuk, Pittenweem still has an active fishing industry (though these days more a flotilla than a fleet). Passing the fish market and the grand historic buildings at the far end of the harbour, walk left up Abbey Road, then

ST MONANS TO CRAIL

◄ St Monans harbour

turn off right on a path beside a housing estate, descending around sea cliffs and skirting the edge of a golf course to enter Anstruther (locally pronounced *Enster*). Originally this was three separate villages, Anstruther Wester, Anstruther Easter and Cellardyke, though they have long since merged.

The coastal path turns left into a residential street, left again, and then right onto the High Street, past the tempting Dreel Tavern and a 16th-century belltower, then across a bridge over the Dreel Burn. Fork right, then immediately turn right again down one of Anstruther's distinctive narrow wynds to reach the sea. In the heyday of the herring fleet, it was said to be possible to walk across the harbour on the close-packed fishing boats.

Shops, cafés and pubs line the seafront, at the far end of which is the award-winning Anstruther Fish Bar and the nearby Scottish Fisheries Museum. Follow James Street east into Cellardyke, once thriving but now a peaceful backwater of 18th-century houses lining a stone harbour.

Beyond an outdoor centre and a caravan park, the coastal path regains open country. After a long level stretch, the route leads past a row of deeply sculpted sandstone stacks and holes, Caiplie Caves, where Irish monk St Aidan was done in by Vikings in about 875AD. Next comes a secluded section beneath gorse-covered banks; passing two ruined cottages, climb over a low headland to enter Crail. A royal burgh since 1310 and one of the finest historic villages in the country, Crail deserves some attention – particularly the Tollbooth, tree-lined Marketgate (once among the largest markets in medieval Europe) and the picturesque stone-walled harbour. Buses run to St Monans and St Andrews from the High Street.

Crail

A917

Caiplie Caves

Anstruther

0 | 2km

Dreel Burn

Scottish Fisheries Museum

B942

Pittenweem

A917

Billow Ness

Monans

windmill

Crail to St Andrews

Distance 20km **Time** 6 hours 30
Terrain rough and remote by local
standards; escapes are limited and several
shoreline sections best negotiated at low
tide; no shelter or refreshments between
Crail and St Andrews **Map** OS Explorer 371
Access from Lower Largo to Crail, all the
East Neuk coastal villages are linked by
buses that run between St Andrews and
Edinburgh or between Leven and St
Andrews; the walk could be cut short at
Kingsbarns or Boarhills

**One of the best and most challenging
walks in Fife, this rugged coastline has a
lonely, unspoilt feel and offers superb
seaside scenery.**

From Crail's High Street, head down
Shoregate, then go left along Castle Street
onto Nethergate, passing handsome 17th-
century houses. Coastal Path signs point

right down a narrow alley, descending
beside a foaming burn to the shore. Turn
left along the sea wall, through a park and
up onto the headland at the east end of
the village. Go through a sprawling
caravan park, entering the more unspoilt
Kilminning Coast Wildlife Reserve by the
natural rock molar of Kilminning Castle.
Beyond patches of dense scrub and a
rocky headland is the coastguard lookout
at breezy Fife Ness.

This is the Kingdom's furthest extremity,
jutting into the open North Sea; from here
the coast swings through ninety degrees,
now leading northwest towards the distant
Angus hills. Pass rocky lagoons, once an
unusual tidal mill, and follow a grassy
marked route around the edge of a golf
course to Constantine's Cave, where –
some say – a Scottish king was slain by
Norse raiders in around 870AD. Loop

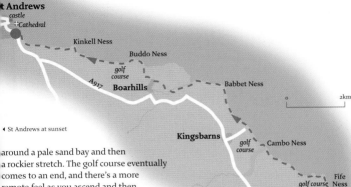

◄ St Andrews at sunset

around a pale sand bay and then a rockier stretch. The golf course eventually comes to an end, and there's a more remote feel as you ascend and then immediately descend to the bottom of the high sandstone cliff of Randerston Castle. Cross the rocky foreshore for a few hundred metres, a stage that's best not done at high tide, before passing a sandy bay. The signed path now skirts yet another golf course, crossing a footbridge over Cambo Burn to reach beautiful Cambo Sands. Follow the edge of the beach to the public car park at its far end.

An obligatory shuffle over soft sand comes next, and might prove tricky at high tide; a marker pole shows where the path regains solid ground. Some 2km or so along the remote rocky coast leads to the mouth of Kenly Water. Instead of fording this broad, fast burn the official route turns inland, following the extremely muddy wooded den to cross a metal footbridge at Burnside Farm. A farm track skirts past Boarhills village (optional escape to a bus stop), passing a doocot to regain the coast at Buddo Rock, a huge free-standing chunk of weathered sandstone.

Now things get rough, with a wild feel despite the nearby golf course. Continuing west, the path zigzags along the coast, sometimes at sea level and sometimes up on the scrubby braes. The cliff scenery is superb, with the spired St Andrews skyline growing gradually closer ahead. There are many flights of stone steps, several very mucky stretches where cattle are grazed, and even at one point the possibility of getting splashed by high waves. About 3km from Buddo Rock is the Rock and Spindle, a famous sea stack. After this, the path climbs to the clifftop for a final leg into St Andrews, passing a caravan park to reach the popular beach at East Sands.

93

Newport-on-Tay to Newburgh

Distance 28km **Time** 8 hours 30
Terrain a mix of tarmac, farm and forest
tracks, and field paths **Maps** OS Explorer
370 and 371 **Access** although both Newport
and Newburgh are accessible by public
transport, getting from one to the other
requires a long journey with at least one
change of bus. An easier alternative is to
leave a car at each end of this linear walk

After a pretty shoreline stretch the Fife
Coastal Path leaves the water, weaving
through peaceful hills above the Firth of
Tay to the historic town of Newburgh.

Follow the High Street and the
continuation of the main B946 through
Newport-on-Tay to Wormit (drivers can do
this by car, saving 3km). Turn right off the
B946 onto Bay Road, following this under
the Tay Rail Bridge to a car park at the end
of the road. From here, follow the Fife
Coastal Path west along the attractive
wooded shore for nearly 4km (as for the
Balmerino loop walk, *page 58*). In Balmerino
turn away from the shore and take the road
straight on past the ruins of Balmerino
Abbey. Turn right at the sign for Newburgh
and follow the road up to the cottages at
Byres. Here, go right onto a track running
below the woods of Coultra Hill for about
2.5km. Turn left at a junction and left again
at the next, climbing to the road at Muir
Dens, where you turn right.

Go straight over the crossroads at
Hazelton Walls and follow the quiet
country road below little hills, passing the
ruined stumps of a castle and church at
Creich. Beyond the hamlet of Brunton turn
right at a T-junction. Just beyond the farm
at Pittachope turn left off the road onto a
track. At a junction go right, following the
track up into a pine plantation. On the left,
the craggy summit of Norman's Law is a
worthwhile detour (*see page 56*). The track